D0394418

BLESS HIS HEART

BY DEBORAH FORD

The GRITS® (Girls Raised in the South) Guide to Life

Puttin' on the GRITS®

GRITS® Friends Are Forevah

BLESS HIS HEART

THE **G**RITS® GUIDE TO LOVING
(OR JUST LIVING WITH) SOUTHERN MEN

Deborah Ford

DUTTON

DUTTON
Published by Penguin Group (USA) Inc.
375 Hudson Street, New York, New York 10014, U.S.A.
Penguin Group (Canada), 90 Eglinton Avenue East, Suite 700, Toronto, Ontario M4P 2Y3, Canada (a division of Pearson Penguin Canada Inc.); Penguin Books Ltd, 80 Strand, London WC2R 0RL, England; Penguin Ireland, 25 St Stephen's Green, Dublin 2, Ireland (a division of Penguin Books Ltd); Penguin Group (Australia), 250 Camberwell Road, Camberwell, Victoria 3124, Australia (a division of Pearson Australia Group Pty Ltd); Penguin Books India Pvt Ltd, 11 Community Centre, Panchsheel Park, New Delhi – 110 017, India; Penguin Group (NZ), cnr Airborne and Rosedale Roads, Albany, Auckland 1310, New Zealand (a division of Pearson New Zealand Ltd); Penguin Books (South Africa) (Pty) Ltd, 24 Sturdee Avenue, Rosebank, Johannesburg 2196, South Africa

Penguin Books Ltd., Registered Offices: 80 Strand, London WC2R 0RL, England

Published by Dutton, a member of Penguin Group (USA) Inc.

First Printing, October 2006
10   9   8   7   6   5   4   3   2   1

 REGISTERED TRADEMARK—MARCA REGISTRADA

LIBRARY OF CONGRESS CATALOGING-IN-PUBLICATION DATA
Ford, Deborah.
  Bless his heart : the GRITS guide to loving (or just living with) southern men /
By Deborah Ford.
    p.   cm.
ISBN 0-525-94971-2 (hardcover)
1. Dating (Social customs) 2. Man-woman relationships. 3. Men—Psychology.
4. Southern States—Humor. I. Title.
HQ801.F65 2006
306.7081'0975—dc22   2006016847

Printed in the United States of America
Set in Adobe Garamond
Designed by Daniel Lagin

While the author has made every effort to provide accurate telephone numbers and Internet addresses at the time of publication, neither the publisher nor the author assumes any responsibility for errors, or for changes that occur after publication. Further, the publisher does not have any control over and does not assume any responsibility for author or third-party Web sites or their content.

This book is dedicated to the memory of my daddy,
William Thornton Rogers.

CONTENTS

ACKNOWLEDGMENTS

I would like to thank all the people who helped make this book possible: Elizabeth Butler Witter, a wonderful writer and friend; my agent, Peter McGuigan; my editors, Trena Keating and Emily Haynes; and to all the wonderful Southern men in my life.

INTRODUCTION

If you're living and breathing in this country, chances are you know a Southern man. And if you're Southern yourself (or just wish you were), chances are you love him. He's chivalrous, kind, and moral, but he can also sure be messy, inattentive, and just plain frustrating.

If you know a Southern man, there are times when you've wondered if he's a plain old Southern man or just plain crazy, and you wish that you had a guide so you can figure out what's going on in that head of his. You love him, bless his heart, but you sure don't understand him.

If any of the following are true of his life, you might need this book:

+ Does he know how to open the door for a lady without stepping on her shoes?
+ Does he know every single word to his school's fight song?
+ Does he sing it at 2 a.m. on the lawn of the opposing team's coach?

✦ Does he think nothing of driving twenty miles to help a friend fix his roof, though he can't make it twenty feet to take the garbage to the curb?

✦ Does he own ten pairs of work pants but not a single tuxedo?

✦ When he comes home, is he often as muddy as the dog trailing along behind him?

✦ Does he love MoonPies, RC Cola, and GooGoo Clusters?

✦ Does he still think Mama can do no wrong, even though he's got grandchildren of his own?

✦ Does he believe that the sole purpose of an oven is to dry out his wet sneakers?

✦ Does he realize that "Ma'am" is not a four-letter word?

As anyone who's ever traded gossip at the beauty parlor knows, there's no better source for information about the Southern man than a Southern woman. I've known and loved a lot of Southern men, and though I don't claim to know everything about them, I've learned a bit in my time. So let's sit down and share a few laughs—and a few groans—about the men who make us crazy, in good ways and bad.

CHAPTER 1

SPOTTING A SOUTHERN MAN IN THE WILD

"Where is the Southern Gentleman, the cultured, polished cavalier with the masculine dash of Rhett Butler, the gallantry of the Tarleton twins, the overbred estheticism of Ashley Wilkes?"

—FLORENCE KING, MISSISSIPPI

"Yes, sir. I'm a real Southern boy. I've got a red neck, white socks, and Blue Ribbon beer."

—BILLY CARTER, GEORGIA

GRITS—Gentlemen Raised in the South, that is— drive Southern girls to distraction. Southern men take off hunting in the middle of the night, making a racket fit to wake the dead. They can't ever seem to remember birthdays or anniversaries, even though they can recall every play Auburn football made in the past fifteen years, including, in depth, each call the referees had wrong. They don't understand why we need to dirty up more than one fork and use the good plates just to serve up supper to the pastor when a plastic spork and a paper plate would do just as well. Those rare times when they discover that their house actually has a kitchen, it looks

DOWN-HOME DICTIONARY

Grits [grĭts] n. (1) *A delicious coarsely ground corn cereal popular throughout the South.* (2) *A man with pride, gentlemanly manners, a love of tradition, and, of course, a charming Southern girl by his side.* (3) *A man who gives you no end of trouble, but who you'll always welcome home anyway.*

like Hurricane Bubba has ransacked the place. No matter how crazy they might make us, though, we can't do without our GRITS. They might exasperate us, poor things, but we know that no matter what kind of foolishness they're up to, their hearts are in the right place.

Who is a Southern gentleman? He's a man in overalls with few words but a lot of wisdom. He's a rough but handsome young thing singing country songs so sad they'd make a statue cry. He's a tough but fair businessman with a strong country accent and stronger down-home common sense. He's a good old boy who's always ready with a drink for his friend, and to take off his hat (or John Deere baseball cap) to any passing lady. He's a well-dressed politician with a handshake for every man and a compliment for every woman. Whether he lives in a tar paper shack in the Tennessee hills or a columned mansion in Houston, he's strong (some might say pigheaded), proud (some might say too big for his britches), and independent (some might say just plain ornery).

MOLASSES AND CORNBREAD

As much as Southern women love to complain about our men, we love them even more than we love our pearls. I hope my own girls, and maybe even their mother, find their own Southern gentlemen to settle down with someday. If life is like a big pan of cornbread, Southern men are the molasses that make it taste so sweet (even if they do mess up the dishes).

✦ *A Southern man is guaranteed to spend less time preening in front of the bathroom mirror than you do.*

✦ Sure, you'll spend more money on fishing rods, power tools, and hunting gear than you would with a Northern man, but you'll spend nothing on psychiatrists and lawyers.

✦ A Southern man knows when to keep his mouth shut. What happens in the home, and certainly what happens in the bedroom, is guaranteed to stay there. When you're married to a Southern man, you don't have to worry about your marital secrets being all over the Internet or, worse, all over Main Street.

✦ He can fix a leaky faucet, change the oil in your car, and raise the best tomatoes you ever tasted, and when you want to go out for a night on the town, he sure cleans up nicely.

✦ That gorgeous Southern drawl first thing in the morning . . . need I say more?

✦ He'll think that you're the most beautiful, fascinating, and intelligent woman on earth . . . next to Mama, of course.

Why am I writing this book? Because I want to honor those dear GRITS and to let them know that, even though they're pains in the neck (and a few other places too), they hold a special place in this Southern girl's heart. But it's not all praise; I want to have a little fun with them, too. I want to let them know that even if we get frustrated when they use our guest towels to wipe motor oil off their hands, and even if we tell our girlfriends about how funny they look when they dress themselves, we still think that they're the most wonderful men in the world.

So how do we go about spotting GRITS in the wild? Well, you can go find a Southern mother and ask where she's sending off her homemade cheese straws, or you can learn how to spot the GRITS among the chaff so you can go out and find one for yourself.

HUNTING CALLS FOR THE SOUTHERN MAN

Hunting for gobblers is easy next to hunting down a Southern man. After all, you can't run down to the local Wal-Mart and bring home a "GRITS-Call." Still, try shouting the following calls (in a ladylike way, of course), and you just might find that a Southern boy answers.

- ✦ *Grits and gravy!*
- ✦ *Deer season!*
- ✦ *Gentlemen, start your engines!*
- ✦ *Ice cold Coca-Cola!*
- ✦ *Well, I do declare, I think this top might be a little tight!*
- ✦ *Play ball!*

STEP 1: THE NAME

A rose by any other name might smell as sweet, but it's hard to imagine a Southern boy named Rainbow or Adolph. Southern parents take naming their children seriously, and Southern boys take almost as much pain in finding a good nickname for their friends. Names tell people who you are and where you came from. If you're introduced to a man named Pierre Beaudreau III you're going to expect someone far different than if you're introduced to a man named "Big Boy" Ferguson.

IT'S THE GOSPEL TRUTH

Elvis Presley left his estate to his beloved daughter, Lisa Marie, but he also left her advice on bringing up her own children: "Be a full-time mom, fill your home with music, raise your child in a stable home, have more than one child, don't neglect your child's spiritual life, insist on a good education, and, if it's a boy, don't name him Elvis."

TRIED AND TRUE SOUTHERN NAMES

If you meet a man with one of these names, there's a good chance he's a Southern boy. If not, well, he's still got a mighty fine name.

Hank . . . as in Williams or Aaron
Clint . . . as in Black
Billy Bob . . . as in Thornton
Jefferson . . . as in Davis
Thomas . . . as in Jefferson
Sonny . . . as in Perdue
Bubba, Skeeter, Catfish, Hoss, Dud, Skinny, Goo-Goo . . . as in
    their poor Mamas never christened them that!

Southerners love the men in their lives so much, they sometimes even name their daughters after them. My daughter was named after a man. Her father, Danny Michael, was working with a dear man, Dr. Chestley Yelton, during my pregnancy. I loved Dr. Yelton, and I loved the name "Chestley." Even though I had a little girl instead of a little boy, I was determined to give her that name, so we dropped the "t" and named her "Chesley."

In the old days, many Southerners would name their children after a beloved relative, or they would turn to the Bible for inspiration. If a Southern family had four boys in a row, there was a good chance they'd be Matthew, Mark, Luke, and John. Parents still value tradition and family in naming their children, and you'll run into a lot of boys with numbers after their names here in the South. Sometimes, we love our relatives so much that we stack several of their names together . . . George Silas Patrick Norton Smith might sound a bit cumbersome to Northerners, but it's just fine to Southern ears. These days, parents are turning to new and creative names, but even if a boy has a new style name, you can tell that he's Southern by listening to his Mama: If she calls him by saying every syllable of his first, middle, and last names, he's a Southern boy.

BEATS ALL I HAVE EVER SEEN!

In 2004, the most popular boy's name in the United States was Jacob. The Southern states of Alabama, Georgia, Mississippi, North Carolina, South Carolina, and Tennessee and the District of Columbia bucked the trend, however, with the most popular name of William (ranking only fourth nationwide). Texas showed a bit of Latin flavor: Its most popular boy's name was José.

A TRUE SOUTHERN GENTLEMEN

Ludlow Porch. When I first heard those words, I thought it was some sort of Southern veranda. You see, I had lived most of my years in Florida, unaware that any human being could possess such a name. However, fate decided that my life was in great need of a make-over and led me to the State of Georgia, home of the Atlanta Braves, The Varsity drive-in, and a radio talk show host named Ludlow Porch. Little did I realize that he was about to drive his red Jasper Jeep into my life and change it forever.

Over the years, I've learned from Ludlow that a true Gentlemen Raised in the South is defined by the words he speaks in addition to the actions he lives. In his professional radio life, Ludlow has often commented, "The microphone is a mirror, a reflection of one's true self, and you cannot hide from it." And every day he reveals the respect and kindness he sincerely feels for all of his listeners, no matter their stations in life. It is an honest indication of the man who sits behind that microphone.

In the business world, Ludlow will be quick to inform any business associate that one should never confuse kindness with weakness. Don't let that soft-spoken Southerner fool you; he's not one to be taken advantage of. In our kitchen at home, we have a plaque on the wall that states, "Blessed are those who are pleasant to live with." It is truly a blessing to live with his kindness and great humor every day.

And when his radio show is almost over, Ludlow ends each broadcast by saying, "Whatever else you do today, you find somebody to be nice to." If you knew him, you'd realize that it's not just something he says, it's the way he lives.

—Nancy Porch,
Georgia

STEP 2: PLUMAGE
AND MARKINGS

The Southern man can be white, black, or, if he's had an arm hanging out of the pickup too long, bright pink. He ranges from rail thin to delicious doughboy. Hair can be high and tight, long and thick like a girl's, business in front and party in the back, or, if he's a well-seasoned GRITS, gone altogether. It's hard to tell a Southern boy by his body, though rugged tanned cheeks and calloused hands are a good indication.

As any Southern girl who's ever dragged a Southern boy kicking and screaming to a black-tie affair can tell you, Southern men don't care much for dressing themselves. When Southern men marry, they're usually perfectly happy to let their wives do the clothes shopping for them, and, before that, they're usually happy to listen to their mothers (even those fifty-year-old bachelors). Southern boys don't want to spend hours in the mall. If they have to shop, it's a commando mission: get in, get out, and hope that no one gets hurt.

If the Southern man has any say in the matter, he prefers simple, comfortable, and sensible clothes. Whoever invented the necktie was not Southern; it's too hot down here for that foolishness. A Southern man would as soon wear his old khakis and a golf shirt every day of the year, and if he doesn't have a woman watching over his shoulder, he just might. If his mother raised him right, he might take the time to wash his clothes (though I wouldn't count on it), but unless there's a woman in his life, don't depend on him pressing anything. As long as the holes aren't in any strategic places, he'll wear the same old thing until it falls right off. That raggedy man with a bad beard walking into the room may be a wonderful GRITS, and a millionaire to boot, just waiting for the right Southern girl to whip him into shape.

No matter how wealthy or worldly they might be, you won't see many Southern men skipping off in the latest silly fashions from Milan or Paris. Southern men dress to fit in, not to stand out. The weather and comfort are more important considerations than fashion.

BEATS ALL I HAVE EVER SEEN!

John Smoltz, pitcher for the Atlanta Braves, once burned himself while ironing a shirt . . . that he was wearing. Said Smoltz: "I couldn't believe it. I've done it five or six times and never had that happen."

If a Southern man manages to find two socks in the same color and to comb his hair, he's a regular fashion fanatic. Don't expect your Southern man to dress elegantly, or to even realize that he shouldn't wear three shades of green at the same time. When it comes to Southern men and fashion, it's best not to aim high. If he cleans the mud off his old boots before going out for the evening, you've got yourself a keeper.

IT'S THE GOSPEL TRUTH

"I wear white socks because I don't have to worry about matching them."
       —Don Sutton, Atlanta Braves announcer
       and Hall of Fame pitcher

You can tell a Southern boy by his colors, or lack thereof. His wardrobe includes khaki, navy, white, and, if he's feeling particularly wacky, a splash of maroon. You might want to show off his sweet baby blues and complement his well-tanned skin, but your Southern man would rather know that he can pull a shirt off the hanger (or, more likely, the floor) and have it match with any pair of slacks he owns. There is one exception, however: hunter orange. The Southern man believes hunter orange goes with everything but church clothes (and a few will try to sneak it in even there). If he owns an orange hunting cap, it's a pretty good giveaway that he's Southern.

STEP 3: THE DRAWL

If you can't tell a Southern man by his appearance or his name, just sit still and listen. That dapper man in the three-piece suit might have manicured hands (no polish, of course!) and gleaming spit-shined shoes, but once he opens his mouth, you can't tell him from the country boy in overalls.

Southern accents differ, of course, and a true Southerner can tell by just a couple of sentences whether you come from a holler in Tennessee or the big city of Nashville. Even with all our differences, however, there's a certain softness, a subtle lilt, in every Southern accent. Southern boys speak slowly and carefully, even if they have only the lightest of accents. Even Southern boys who have been away from home for too long find themselves slipping back into a Southern drawl when they talk about the first buck they bagged.

SAY WHAT?

If you haven't got the time to develop a linguistic map of the South, just give him the following test:

✦ Say: "Cold fried chicken sure is greasy." "Greasy" rather than "greazy" is a dead giveaway that he's a Yankee—and that his poor Mama can't make good fried chicken to save her life.

✦ Have him complete the following sentence: "On a hot day, there's nothing like a tall, cold glass of _____." If he says "pop" or "soda," he's not a Southern boy. If he says "Coke" or "beer," he's from the South; if he says "iced tea," drag that boy off to the altar as fast as you can.

✦ Complete the following: "Me, myself, and ____." A Southern boy will say "ah" rather than "aye."

✦ Ask him to say "Miss" and "Ms." If he pronounces them the same way, chances are he's Southern, and if he tips his hat to you as he says it, chances are every woman within ten feet will swoon.

✦ No matter how he pronounces his words, if anything he says is sweeter than honey and slower than molasses, you know you've got yourself a Southern boy.

DOWN-HOME DICTIONARY

metaphor [mĕt ə fôr] n. (1) A figure of speech in which something usually used to designate one thing is used to designate another. "Earl ain't nothing but a hound dog." (2) Having been acquainted with someone previously. "Do you know Earl?" "Yup, I think we've metaphor."

UNCLE ABE'S APHORISMS
AND TRUE SAYINGS

My father earned the nickname "Uncle Abe" for being as honest as Abraham Lincoln. He was the only person I knew who admitted voting for "Big Jim" Folsom, the legendarily colorful governor of Alabama. Growing up in rural North Carolina during the early 1900s, my father's formal education was cut off at the tenth grade. Still, he had his own wisdom, and his aphorisms were, to say the least, interesting.

"Grinnin' like a mule eatin' briars." Without further explanation, I refer you to Jimmy Carter.

"Mean as a striped snake." Also, without explanation, see Senator Joseph McCarthy.

"Looks like a dog shook." What I heard when I stepped out of the shower, dripping wet.

"Living off the interest of what they owe." Folks who put up a front of affluence but are living one paycheck from bankruptcy.

"Boring with a big auger." Folks who are living off the interest of what they owe.

"Folks aren't supposed to act like rabbits running in the field." As close as Uncle Abe could get to telling us about the birds and the bees.

"Makes you want to go home and kill your boy." After hearing a coworker talk about the achievements of his son.

"So lazy the dead lice fall off." He apparently knew some folks who were seriously lacking in ambition.

"You'll look like where a cat ate a lizard . . . there'll be only a greasy spot left." His warning to me to stay off of highways and out of airplanes.

—Carlton Martin,
Alabama

STEP 4: HIS RAISING (UPBRINGING, THAT IS)

If nothing else will give it away, you can always identify a GRITS by how he acts. His neighbors might grumble about him and his rowdy friends, his wife might mutter about the weeds that are higher than the house, and his poor mother might faint at the sight of the deer strung up in the front yard, but no matter how crazy he might make us, he won't forget his manners. When I was a child, no Southern man would dream of letting a woman fix her own flat tire. He might be late for work, his best friend might have just landed the record bass for the county, or he might be rushing off to meet the pretty little woman in his own life, but any Southern man worth his grits would pull over and help a woman in need. He knew that she could change it herself, maybe even faster than he could, if need be—no Southern man could grow up around Southern women and not respect their strength and resourcefulness— but he saw in that woman in distress his mother, his girlfriend, his wife, and his sister.

BEATS ALL I HAVE EVER SEEN!

Do Southern men have a stronger sense of honor? Researchers have found that Southern men tend to react more strongly to an unprovoked insult from a stranger than Northern men. When insulted, the levels of stress hormones and testosterone increased in Southern men and stayed the same in Northern men.

IT'S THE GOSPEL TRUTH

"Even though my husband is sixteen years my senior, when we met, he was a bit timid. When we started dating, he asked me if he could kiss me. When I said yes, he kissed me on the cheek. I knew he was a keeper!"

—Roberta Moss, Texas

PHONE MANNERS

I love Southern men for so many reasons, but I mostly love the way they treat women.

I once worked in the customer service department of the Columbus, Mississippi, company Motorguide, a manufacturer of trolling motors. I rarely talked to happy fishermen. If you want to make any fisherman really grumpy, just mess with his trolling motor.

I could always tell the difference between the angry Southern men and the angry Yankees. Angry Yankee men would cuss me up one side and down the other—often hurling insults as though I had personally flown to their houses and messed with their trolling motors. Southern men, on the other hand, were always careful about their language and about whether they made personal attacks on me. "Now, honey, I know this isn't your fault . . ." they'd always begin before laying out their troubles. If a cuss word slipped out, they always apologized profusely. The way those Southern men talk not only made my job a lot easier, it also made me proud of the South.

—L. Sargent,
Alabama

Now, don't get me wrong, it isn't all chivalry and roses with Southern boys. After all, we're the region of courtly manners, but we're also the region of hot rodding, beer drinking, good old boys with oil under their fingernails. The difference between Northern and Southern country boys, however, is that while a Southern boy can cuss with the best of them, he always keeps a civil tongue when a lady is around; after all, he may not fear hunting wild boar, but he doesn't want to face down an angry Southern girl. Whether it's his mother or his wife, a GRITS knows that if he doesn't watch his mouth, there's a woman around to watch it for him.

THE OTHER "F" WORD

I turned thirteen in 1956, a time in the South when public decency reigned supreme, and a man's word was his bond, even possibly indicative of the spiritual condition of his soul. Important words beginning with "F" were faith, family, and friends—until the day I heard for the first time another "F" word.

Dad had bought a new Chevy Bel Air coupe with fender skirts, chrome drip caps, and a chrome tissue dispenser for Mom that could hide beneath the dashboard. We all loaded into the car, including Granny, who could get car sick just riding the one mile to town. On Saturdays in small Southern towns, stores were full of customers, sidewalks a beehive of pedestrians, and streets were full of automobiles in increasing numbers.

Careful with his new car, Dad had started his right turn onto Market Street when brakes squealed and horns blew. A car had turned left into our lane, almost crashing into our shiny new car. With Dad's fiery nature, the instant boil of red in his face said it all. The only time I'd seen him that angry was when we caught Berkley Taylor, drunk as usual, peeping in a window. I thought Dad was going to literally crawl out the car window. With half his body hanging out the window, he shouted, "What the f*** are you doing, Mister! You tryin' to kill us all?"

While Mom lowered her head in embarrassment, Granny, truly an old saint with anything but a scornful spirit, was instantly incensed. Her eyes widened, her face flashed pickled beet red, and the only thing that contained her words were her lips so tightened they looked like a thread. Her eyes drilled Dad.

"Stop this very instant and let me out. I'm not listening to any such vulgarity, not for a single minute. I don't tolerate it from strangers, and I'm not about to tolerate it from my own son."

Dad pulled the car to the curb at her wish.

"What does that word mean, Mom?" I asked nervously.

She explained it to be a word that should never fall from the lips of decent people, especially Christians, that Dad's flesh had gotten the best of him. Having been beaten up in an alley by a school bully and his three cronies weeks earlier, and having used a few choice words of my own, I understood perfectly.

"Mom, I'm sorry. Please wait," Dad said, leaving the car, his words fading as he followed Granny up the street apologizing, and in front of the whole world. Stunned by the realization that no manner of explanation, or apology, could change her mind, he returned to the car, slumped in failure, rubbing his forehead as if he had a major headache. I knew the feeling. My words in the alley had driven the most beautiful girl I had ever seen, and wanted to know better, away after she had come to my rescue.

Mom raised her brow. "Bud?" she queried firmly.

"I'm sorry, son. I shouldn't have let that idiot get the best of me." Persuasion gripped him. *"But hon, we all could've been killed!"*

"Bud?" Mom repeated, calmly.

Dad yielded with a subdued sigh. "But I was wrong, son. Lord forgive me."

Dad was a man of faith who worked hard, minded his own business, and was crazy about his family. After that Saturday, I never heard him say that word again, any word remotely kin, or, for that matter, any word that came close to being considered vulgar.

If that were Dad's only sin, then he's a far better man than most, including myself. Sometime thereafter, I asked Granny how she felt about the incident. Her reply was simply, "Son, all sin and come short of the glory of God."

—*Willis Baker,*
Tennessee

Southern men aren't brought up to weep over the soap operas, but don't get them wrong, they're still feeling. Chip away at that tough exterior, and you'll find a sweet, sentimental heart. He may not be a touchy-feely Northern liberal, but any fool can listen to a country radio station for ten minutes and know that, in his heart, a Southern boy is as soft as a pussycat and as sweet as a puppy. He may not advertise his feelings, or even admit to having them, but, sometimes, when you catch him singing a sad old country song in his pickup, you'll catch a little tear running down that rugged face.

A SOUTHERN WEDDING

Most people think that at weddings the women are the emotional ones. Not in my family. Maybe it was because it was the first family wedding in twenty years, but when my daughter was married, it was the men of the family who cried. My husband cried as he was walking his baby down the aisle. My son-in-law cried as he said his vows. My son cried when he danced with his sister. My own Daddy cried during the ceremony. My brother-in-law got sentimental, telling my daughter that if there was anything at all she needed, she shouldn't hesitate to call. The bride was the one person who did not shed a tear all day.

When my husband went to dance with my daughter, the DJ announced: "For twenty-two years Mark has had two brown-eyed girls, and tonight he gives one to Jason." He then played "Brown-Eyed Girl." By the end of the song, my husband was crying so hard that he was not even able to finish the dance.

My son commented later how the whole day was all about family, and I think he was right. You can't have family without a few tears, of joy and pain, and our Southern men are men enough to cry right along with our women.

—Kathy Neno,
Alabama

STEP 5: THE DAWG

If you're in doubt about whether a man is Southern, look down; chances are a dog is trailing along beside him. He's dirty, he's smelly, and he never seems to come when you call . . . and his dog could use some training as well! If you want a

Southern man, you're going to have to want, or at least put up with, his dog.

Fortunately, most Southern women love dogs, but if you're that rare exception that doesn't, realize that his dog is more than an animal: It's a best buddy. You're a special little pearl, honey, but his dog also has an important place in his heart. You wouldn't want a man who would throw over his best friend for someone else, so be proud that he loves his dog. Sometimes, adjusting is difficult, especially when your sweet little Persian runs and hisses every time his big old hound enters the room, but anything worthwhile is worth working for. Don't worry, even if you don't love that big animal at first, he'll quickly melt your heart. You have to love someone who nuzzles you every time you walk in the door, and who howls every time you leave—and, given a little time, you'll find that his dog isn't so bad either!

His dog has full command of the house, the truck, and the yard—and most of the time he hasn't done a thing to deserve it. In the old days, dogs earned their keep around the house. They put meat on the table by helping their masters on the hunt. They protected the families during the long nights when the nearest neighbors were a mile away and there was no such thing as 911. Still today, many Southern dogs are working dogs, but even if they aren't, they've earned a valuable place in the Southern man's heart.

DOWN-HOME DICTIONARY

dawg ['dȯ ag] *A Southern boy's best friend, preferably big, slobbery, and friendly. Poodles and Chihuahuas might be "dogs," but they'll nevah, evah, be "dawgs."*

BEATS ALL I HAVE EVER SEEN!

Southern men love their dogs so much that they honor them even when they've passed. A rural road near Tuscumbia, Alabama, is home to the famous Coon Dog Graveyard. In 1937, Key Underwood buried his dog, Troop, on the plot. Since then, roughly 200 dogs have been buried in this cemetery. Only the best coon dogs are eligible to be buried there, so don't even bother asking about a final resting place for Ms. Fluffy.

IT'S THE GOSPEL TRUTH

Next to his dog, duct tape is a Southern man's best friend.

IT'S THE GOSPEL TRUTH

"If you pick up a starving dog and make him prosperous, he will not bite you. That is the difference between dog and man."
—Mark Twain, Missouri GRITS

DOG TRAINING

How do you treat a man? Maybe you should take a course in dog training.

❖ *Ask for what you want clearly. Often women are afraid of driving men away, so they try to hide their true wishes and feelings. Neither dogs nor men are good at understanding conflicting signals, and the men aren't very good at understanding any kind of signal at all. If you want either of them to stop lying around, shedding on your couch, say so kindly but also firmly.*

❖ *Use rewards abundantly. Man and dog alike can't resist petting from a Southern woman.*

❖ *Get him out of the house. He's got plenty of energy, and if you don't watch it, he'll channel that into destruction (or if he's a man, home "improvement"). If you don't want your furniture torn to bits, get him outdoors frequently.*

❖ *Playtime. The key is to increase attention span and attachment, not to change his basic character. You liked him for his frisky and fun nature when you met, so let him play.*

IT'S THE GOSPEL TRUTH

Choosing a name for your best friend is an important responsibility. Southern men often name their dogs after friends, family members, or even favorite politicians or celebrities. Besides Rex or Lucky, you're just as likely to find Bocephus, Lady Bird, or General Lee.

IT'S THE GOSPEL TRUTH

Lewis Grizzard's love for his dog Catfish was legendary. While Catfish wasn't perfect—he's known to have chewed up everything from two whole chickens to a complete set of patio furniture—his love and loyalty made up for his faults. When he passed on, Mr. Grizzard wrote: "Now he has up and died. My own heart, or what is left of it, is breaking."

WHY SOUTHERN BOYS ARE LIKE THEIR DOGS

✦ *Both are loyal. Even when all you want is a bit of peace, they'll be right along at your side, rubbing up against your ankles.*

✦ *They both work hard and won't give up until the job is done, even if that "job" is chasing squirrels all day. And when quitting time comes, both know there's nothing better than a well-earned rest under the shade of their favorite tree.*

✦ *No matter what the women and the cardiologists might tell them, both know that there's nothing finer than a juicy piece of meat, though Southern men liked theirs cooked, preferably over an open fire in the great outdoors.*

✦ *You'll never catch either wearing a fluffy sweater or being carried around in a pink leather purse.*

IT'S THE GOSPEL TRUTH

When you're getting a dog, you're making a commitment for the rest of the life of that animal. That means brisk walks even in the dead of February, dog hair on everything from the living room sofa to your best coat, and your best pair of pumps becoming a chew toy. Before you and the man in your life bring an animal into your home, be sure that the two of you agree on walking and feeding schedules, discipline, and sleeping arrangements.

IT'S THE GOSPEL TRUTH

Some nights, it seems like that smelly old hound dog has more room in the bed than you and your husband combined. Asking him to sleep on the floor, or even outside, may be too much to ask of your husband's best friend, but insisting that the dog be clean and free of fleas is perfectly acceptable. After a while, you'll learn to expect and even want that old fleabag in your bed (the dog, that is, not your husband!). When nights get chilly, you'll be glad that old Rufus is curled up at your feet.

STEP 6: THE CAR

You can tell GRITS by the pride he takes in his car, and by the casual skill (some might say recklessness) with which he drives it. Southern men love their cars. Even if all a GRITS can afford is a beat-up Gremlin, that piece of rust holds a special place in his heart. In the South, a man and his car are like a cowboy and his horse, and even if it's a gray old nag, he's going to treasure it. All over the South, you'll see the saddest double-wides, hanging on to dear life with nothing but a little duct tape and caulking, but out back there's a polished muscle car, a V-8 under the hood and polished leather on the seats. A car is to a Southern man what a hair dryer is to a Southern woman; sure, it's just a machine, but it's one he'd nevah, evah, do without. We might wish that they'd forget that car for long enough to take out the garbage or rake the lawn, but they're only men, poor things, and they just can't help themselves around an engine.

You can't judge a Southern boy by the condition of his vehicle. One school of Southern guys treats their cars like newborn babies, washing them carefully, checking and rechecking under the hood, and buffing the paint to a high sheen. Messing with their cars is messing with their pride and joy. Then there is the school that takes pride in how much abuse that good old American-made piece of machinery can take. Even though the truck bed might look like a biology experiment, don't wash it; all that mud just might be what's holding it together.

BEATS ALL I HAVE EVER SEEN!

Fifty-five percent of men admit to talking to their cars. Now, if we could just get that many men to talk about their feelings, there'd be no need for Dr. Phil!

IT'S THE GOSPEL TRUTH

"This car is like a beautiful woman in a bar—every guy goes up to it."
—Kevin Costner, on his Mustang

IT'S THE GOSPEL TRUTH

We think men buy cars to impress the girls, but, in reality, impressing the other guys is even more important.

We all know that even though they may tool around town in a top-of-the-line Lexus or BMW, GRITS all secretly hanker after a pickup. He'll be sitting behind the wheel of his luxury car, and out of the corner of his eye, he'll spot a Chevy or a Ford idling beside him, and he'll sigh wistfully, picturing days hauling around supplies for his suburban lawn or a truck bed full of hunting dogs. Someone once told me that Charlotte, North Carolina, was a town full of "bankers with pickups." He might not have intended that as a compliment, but the women of Charlotte, like the women throughout the South, can look at the men with pride; no matter how successful they might become, you can't get the Southern soil out of their hearts.

IT'S THE GOSPEL TRUTH

"I'm married to Felicity Huffman, who is a babe, so normally guys stare at her. But if we're in my truck, they stare at the truck."
—William H. Macy, Florida GRITS, on his 1952 Chevy truck

BEATS ALL I HAVE EVER SEEN!

Longview, Texas, is home to the annual "Hands on a Hardbody" contest. The contest's title might lead you to think that something ungentlemanly was happening, but don't worry, it's just a contest to win a hardbody truck. Contestants must stand, day and night, with one hand on the truck they're trying to win. Contestants are not permitted to lean on the truck, and anyone who removes a hand is out of the running. The last man (or woman) standing wins the truck. Contestants have lasted as long as one hundred and twenty-six hours—or more than five days!

Just because Southern men love their cars doesn't mean that you can always trust one behind the wheel. Every GRITS has his unique driving style, and, unfortunately, that rarely means one hand at eleven and one at two o'clock. You can take a perfectly nice Southern boy, a sweet accountant who goes to church on Sunday and greets his grandmother with a kiss on the cheek, and the minute he gets behind the wheel, he's in his own personal Indy 500. Or maybe he still acts as though he's picking his way down a rut-filled country road, even though cars are whizzing around him on the interstate. Either way, I'd never have anyone but a Southern man as my mechanic, but I'd as soon walk as have one as a chauffeur.

STEP 7: FEEDING TIME

A Southern man loves food, sometimes a little too much than is good for his waistline, as every Southern wife can tell you. The Southern man prefers the simple, fresh, and bold flavors of his childhood. He respects a cook who can make a perfect bowl of red beans and rice far more than one who spends hundreds of dollars chasing the latest food trend. Down in the South, food is still regional. You'll find jambalaya in Louisiana, cornbread and butterbeans in the Piedmont, dry-rub barbecue in Memphis, shrimp and grits in the low country, and a bowl of red in Texas. One thing that all Southern food has in common is that it is traditional, and, preferably, made by a Southern grandmother at home. Southern men crave the tastes of their childhood, whether that means dirty rice or Frito pie. What matters is that the flavors are down-home and good to the last bite.

BEATS ALL I HAVE EVER SEEN!

Sales of pork rinds, that staple of Southern gas stations and general stores, rose 37 percent between 2002 and 2003. Many credit the success of low-carb diets with putting a taste of the South into everyone's mouth.

Southern men don't have much patience with the newfangled, and sometimes just plain strange, food you find in fancy restaurants. You might be disappointed if you try out a new recipe on him, but at least you know that he won't turn up his nose at the old favorites. If you see a man digging in to a heaping plate of greens with pepper vinegar, hot cornbread, and field peas, chances are you're looking at a Southern man. If you see a man ordering a plate of frog legs with kumquat jelly, he's probably not a Southerner . . . and you better hand the poor dear an antacid.

While Southern men like to eat, it seems like the poor sweethearts can't locate anything in the kitchen but a six-pack or the leftover wings, and, after repeated calls for help as they stand in front of the open icebox, I'm not even sure they can do that much. Sure, they're pretty good over a camp stove or a backyard grill, but give them a saucepan and a whisk, and suddenly they're as helpless as a bass flopping around on the bottom of the boat. There are a few exceptions, of course, and if you find them, by all means, snap them up, but, by and large, if you want to be with a Southern man, you'd better learn to cook (or, better yet, to dial for take-out!).

RENAISSANCE MAN

I call my husband of thirty-six years my "Renaissance Man." He has his "manly" pursuits of hunting, fishing, and driving his tractor, but he also has another side. He grows roses with exotic names such as "Taboo," "Sultry," and "Rio Samba," and when you see and smell their beauty, you realize that the names don't do them justice. After I get a big bouquet for my table, our daughter, daughter-in-law, granddaughters, mother-in-law, coworkers, and neighbors get some, too. He is always happy to share.

He does about half the cooking in our house. After he found out that my favorite dish is shrimp, he leaned to boil, fry, and sauté them. His shrimp pasta is just heavenly. There's nothing like coming home from work on a cold night and smelling his cooking.

He learned to make biscuits from the mother of one of his deer camp buddies. She would make them and bring them over to the camp for the guys. One afternoon, he went over to her house and asked if she would please teach him to make them. Of course, she was flattered and more than happy to teach him. He does all the things we keep men around for: mowing the yard, fixing things, hanging pictures . . . and some things that I won't discuss in public! But he's very good at those things, too.

Being a man, he's certainly not perfect, but he's close enough for me. I've been in love with him since I was sixteen years old. My Southern man makes me feel loved, protected, and cherished. When you really think about it, what more could you ask for?

—Pam McCollough,
Mississippi

BEATS ALL I HAVE EVER SEEN!

While it seems that the Southern boys in most women's lives don't know a marinade from a mariachi, it isn't just women in the kitchen in the new South. Food is a passion in the South for men and women alike. Southern men know that top-quality, creative cooking is a manly profession, and they aren't hiding their talents. Chef Scott Peacock of Atlanta focuses on Southern cuisine, and he uses fresh, seasonal ingredients to make food that nourishes the body and the soul. He's written a book, The Gift of Southern Cooking: Recipes and Revelations from Two Great American Cooks, with his friend Edna Lewis, the woman who helped popularize Southern cooking nationwide. Birmingham chef Frank Stitt's Highlands Bar & Grill was named one of the top five restaurants in the United States by Gourmet magazine. And just about everyone in the country has said "Bam!" along with Louisiana's Emeril Lagasse.

STEP 8: A LITTLE BIT COUNTRY, A LITTLE BIT ROCK-AND-ROLL

It used to be that you could tell a Southern boy by the red on his neck and the dirt under his fingernails (at least until his wife found out and made him scrub), but, these days, he's just as likely to be a city boy. Sure, he'll always have a bit of the country in his heart, but he's just as likely to know how to close a big deal or design a building as to tune up a tractor.

IT'S THE GOSPEL TRUTH

Even the most successful Southern man dreams of home when work carries him far away. Says the Chairman of the Media and Communications Group, Time Warner: "I'm a sucker for coming back home. . . . As soon as I'm back, I'm eating barbecue—there's no good barbecue in New York . . . you never forget your roots if you're a Southerner. We like to go back home and curl up in our nest."

—Don Logan,
New York

AN ALABAMA BOYHOOD

My Mom and Dad separated shortly after the birth of my youngest brother. With six boys to take care of, Mom had to watch every nickel. Although Dad sent money almost every week from his construction job up North, we never had what you would call a comfortable income.

We all chopped cotton when it was first planted, and, later, we all helped to pick it. Farmer Childers from Warrior, Alabama, always enjoyed having us six boys and my mother work for him. When we started picking cotton the first of the season, we were paid four cents a pound. As the season wore on, cotton became more plentiful on the market, and Farmer Childers couldn't pay as much. At the end of the picking season it paid only two and a half cents a pound. We went from four dollars for a hundred pounds at the beginning of the season to two and a half dollars at the end.

Cotton picking would not be enough to hold us over and feed the family, so we all pitched in to make extra money. When I was about twelve years old, I started going around to all the houses in the Seloca (pronounced 'slo kee) neighborhood near Warrior gathering "Coke" bottles (every soda, even RC, was "Coke" back then). I would load them all in my Western Flyer red wagon and take them to the combination service station and store for the drink trucks. Back then, no one charged a deposit on the bottles unless you were from out of town and passing through. Otherwise, it was understood that you would be bringing the bottles back. People never did seem to get around to making their returns, though, so I was employed to go around and pick them up once a week. The neighbors all put their empties out on the back porch where I could find them.

I left Warrior after high school graduation and went "up North" to join my dad in construction. I rose through the ranks, and, later, I was lucky enough to return to the South. I think I owe my drive to all that hard work I did growing up, and, though it was hard sometimes, I wouldn't trade my Alabama boyhood for anything in the world.

—Dennis Hardiman,
Georgia

GUIDE TO GRITS CHEAT SHEET

Southern	Not Southern
Y'all	Youse guys
Football	Field hockey
Tight-fitting jeans	Leather pants
Biscuits and gravy	Dry toast
"Pardon me, ma'am"	"Hey, lady, watch it!"
Hardbody	Low rider
Barber	Stylist

CHAPTER 2

RULES OF THE ROAD

"The only time a woman really succeeds in changing a man is when he is a baby."

—NATALIE WOOD

"Courtesy is as much a mark of a gentleman as courage."

—THEODORE ROOSEVELT, NEW YORK (BUT IT'S CLEAR HIS MOTHER, BORN IN ROSWELL, GEORGIA, WAS A TRUE SOUTHERN LADY!)

Steering a Southern man isn't always easy. If he's like a car, he sure doesn't come equipped with power steering. Getting him to go in the right direction sometimes takes a little tug-of-war. Southern men don't take too kindly to nagging, or even to gentle direction; they're too independent for that. Talking to them, we sometimes feel that we might as well be shouting into the wind. It's possible to get along with Southern men, however, and even get them to change directions occasionally; you just have to know the rules of the road.

IT'S THE GOSPEL TRUTH

"Men are like a fine wine. They start out like grapes, and it's our job to stomp on them and keep them in the dark until they mature into something you'd like to have dinner with."

—*Anonymous*

Even though they're stubborn as mules, and often twice as ornery, GRITS are worth the trouble. I like to think of Southern men the way I think of a good pair of high heels. When we put on our first pair, we wobbled, and they took some getting used to. We kicked them off and swore that we'd never put ourselves through that trouble again. There've been instances when we've caught our heels in cracks or grates, and we've stumbled and even fallen. At the end of the night, our poor little soles sometimes cried out for relief.

But that doesn't mean we don't love them! High heels are sometimes hard to walk in, just like Southern men are sometimes a bit tetchy, but it just means that we have to take more delicate steps when we deal with either. Although we had some trouble in our heels at first, soon our walk became far more glamorous and graceful for wearing them, just as we feel more beautiful beside our men. We love our high heels, and

BEATS ALL I HAVE EVER SEEN!

Believe it or not, Southern girls did not invent high heels. In the fifteenth to seventeenth centuries, European women wore high-heeled, platformed shoes known as chopines, which could reach the dizzying height of thirty inches. These enormous shoes were worn over slippers and were meant to keep the hems of dresses out of the mud that then coated the streets. Practicality gave way to fashion, however, and the shoes became so high that women wearing them would need the help of a servant to keep from toppling over. Next time your husband complains about your delicate gait in stilettos, just tell him that he's lucky you didn't pick out a pair of chopines.

we wouldn't trade either our men or our heels for all the sneakers DSW has to offer. Why? High heels—and very fine Southern gentlemen—make every woman look better.

We sometimes struggle with our GRITS, wondering why on earth they spend so much time in the garage and so little time planning our anniversary party. We just can't understand why they can drone on about sports for longer than the actual game when we can't get them to say five words about their feelings. We shake our heads over the fact that he can remember the name of every part of his truck's engine, but he can't remember to change the air-conditioner filter once a month. We have to struggle to get him dressed up for a big night out, and, bless his heart, sometimes we give up and just go with the girls.

IT'S THE GOSPEL TRUTH

You don't break in a pair of new shoes by cutting the heels and toes off, you stretch and soften the leather gently by wearing them. One of the things we love about our Southern men is their pride, so a Southern lady wouldn't dream of nitpicking her husband in public. If you must criticize your husband, do so in private, and do so gently. Show at least the same respect for the men in your life that you do to your shoes, and the two of you will soon fit like your favorite three-inch Italian heels.

Once you break a Southern man in, he can be a friend you can love for years. My good friend Ed Williams is one such man.

FRIENDSHIP JUST DOESN'T GET ANY BETTER THAN THIS

Most of us men enjoy good friendships, although we don't talk about it a whole lot, for two reasons:

1. If you get into deep, spiritual discussions about your closest male friends, some people tend to arch an eyebrow and wonder if you like to embroider doilies or watch one of the shopping channels on cable TV.

2. If you happen to be married or engaged and get into deep, spiritual discussions about your closest female friends, you might find yourself suddenly homeless or without certain body parts that you'd much like to continue having.

All that being said, I'm still gonna talk about friendships, 'cause I've got two of the best friendships goin' on in the South today, and that's with my two friends, Miss Deborah Ford (or "Miss GRITS," as I like to call her) and Dedra Grizzard (widow of the late, great Mr. Lewis Grizzard).

That's right, I'm lucky enough to be good friends with both Miss GRITS and Dedra Grizzard. I hang out with 'em much of the time, and enjoy it more than two free front-row tickets to the World Toughman Championships. All of you guys out there can start eating your hearts out about it right now, and I wouldn't blame y'all one bit for doing so. But that's the way it is, so learn to love it. And, after all the cussin' and *teeth grindin', y'all might just be asking yourselves, how did this Ed guy get so lucky?*

Well, I'm not quite sure why myself, but I'm not fightin' it. And some things about it add right up, if you really think about it. Miss GRITS, Dedra, and I are all true, genetic Southerners, which means that we all speak the same language, like most of the same foods, and appreciate the fact that Elvis, Jerry Lee, and Buddy Holly all come from the South. We enjoy a good laugh together, appreciate strength of character, and aren't above gobbling down a good Varsity or Nu-Way chili dog if the chance presents itself. We like hot weather, cold drinks, and boiled peanuts when the time is right. Only a true, genetic Southerner really understands and appreciates a good boiled peanut.

I get sympathy from Miss GRITS and Dedra when I get homesick on the road. I get to hash out things with them, maybe sipping drinks by the side of the pool. If either Miss GRITS or Dedra buys a stunning new dress or swimsuit, and happens to want an opinion about it, I get to stare at them and get into absolutely no trouble for doing so.

Now do y'all understand why these friendships are so special? And why friendships can't get any better than this? It ought to be more obvious than a rhino dressed in a tutu. The three of us just enjoy each other's company, and we're committed to havin' more fun together and makin' our friendships even stronger.

—Ed Williams,
Georgia

NEW ETIQUETTE
FOR THE GOOD OLD BOY

I can't help hurting for our dear GRITS. I know from experience that Southern men can't keep more than one thing in their cute little heads at a time. At the sight of a running back—not to mention a cheerleader—on television, all thoughts of cleaning up that messy "project" he's been working on for three months slip his mind. Wave a power saw in front of them, and they'll completely forget their boss is coming over tonight. And don't even think about asking them to wash the car and take care of the yard; chances are the car will be soaped up, the hedges will be half trimmed, and your man, bless his heart, will have wandered off to discuss bass fishing with the next door neighbor.

How do we expect these poor dears to keep modern etiquette straight? There was a time when knowing the rules of the road was easy. A man stood when a lady entered the room, held out his date's chair, and carried the packages of an elderly woman. Women smiled and accepted the man's help graciously. These days, men don't know what to do, and women don't know whether to accept a man's assistance or toss their heads and say "no, thank you."

MALE CHAUVINISTS

The older generation of men in my family were typical Southern men, and chauvinists to the core. They truly believed that they had to protect women. But they also prided themselves on being wiser and more intelligent than any woman. No matter what the men thought, though, I realize now that it was the women in the family who kept things going. They raised the children, ran the homes, took care of the men, and, of course, spoiled them outrageously.

My father was schooled by his uncles and great-uncles in the ways of Southern manhood. When it became his responsibility to raise two sons and three daughters without a mother in the house, he was determined that I—the oldest girl—would keep the house running, wait on him, and assume responsibility for my sisters and brothers, all of whom were within six years of my age.

In spite of the responsibility he placed on such a young girl's shoulders, there was never any question that he cared for us. Despite the fact that our father was president of many organizations, was on the Vestry at the Episcopal Cathedral of the Advent, and owned his own business, he never missed a single recital, ball game, school function, or religious ceremony when any of us were involved.

My father wasn't much for gifts or grand gestures. Like most men I've known, it was the simple things that spoke volumes about his heart. When I made my confirmation in my church, he gave me a beautiful corsage, and I was the only girl in church that day wearing something so beautiful. It might seem like a small thing to some people, but, for me, it's a special memory that I'll always treasure. My father felt that I was important and unique, and he wanted for me to shine above those other girls. It let me know that he didn't see me just as someone to take care of him. Chauvinist or not, my father loved me, and he let me know how special I was.

—Catherine Greene Browne,
Alabama

Southern men mean well, even if they seem as old-fashioned as an eight-track tape player. When he performs a small courtesy, such as holding my chair, or a larger one, such as helping me with a stalled car, the Southern man is doing me the honor of noticing that I'm a woman. He realizes that I'm a different creature—genetically predisposed to love shopping, Oprah, and a fine whine—and he loves me for it.

LIVING THE OLD WAYS IN THE NEW WORLD

When there's a sea of men out there, but no GRITS to throw you a life preserver, you just might wonder what the world's coming to. Don't worry, honey, it's still possible to convert some of those other sorry old dogs.

✦ *Don't automatically assume that the behavior you see is rudeness just because it isn't the behavior you grew up with. In a crowded shopping mall, thousands of people pass each other each day, so waving and saying hello to each one is impossible, not to mention looking a bit teched. Walking side-by-side with all your friends might be just the neighborly thing to do in a small town or a quiet suburban street, but on the congested sidewalks of a big city, it blocks other pedestrians and is downright uncivil.*

✦ *It may be that the men around you are behaving badly because they think women like and expect it. Some men tell stories that would make a fishwife blush, and they keep it up in front of women because they are trying to treat them as equals. Meet incivility with graciousness, bad language with fine manners.*

When men see that you're behaving like a lady, they might fall in line naturally.

✦ *If he doesn't respond, state your criticisms in the politest way possible. "It's interesting how things are so different when you travel. Where I come from, a man wouldn't use that word in front of a lady," is certainly preferable to "watch your tongue, you young whippersnapper!" If your kind response doesn't have him blushing and stammering an apology, let him behave however he wants; he isn't a GRITS and he's not worth the trouble.*

HOW TO IMPRESS THE SOUTHERN GENTLEMAN

Sometimes, Southern women fret so much about how Southern men have let their manners go to the dogs that we forget that we have the same responsibility to keep things up. You can't have a belle without her beau, and a world of Southern gentlemen isn't much fun unless there are some ladies around, too. For every Southern man I see wearing his hat in a movie theater, I see a Southern woman on her cell phone discussing at the top of her lungs things that would make her mother blush. For every Southern man that I see bursting through a door without waiting for the woman behind him, I see a Southern woman let someone who looks like her grandmother struggle through with a load of packages.

FIVE WAYS TO A
SOUTHERN BOY'S HEART

Winning over a Southern boss, beau, or neighbor is easy. Just keep five simple rules in mind, and you'll be as welcome as a Dallas Cowboys cheerleader toting a plate of ribs.

1. *Knowledge. Know who your people are and where they came from. Learn how to make a good plate of fried chicken and biscuits that melt in your mouth. Learn how to run a trout line and, even better, how to clean your catch. Know how to hoe, weed, and tend a garden. Learn the lyrics of at least three Willie Nelson songs. Know the basic rules of football, baseball, and NASCAR.*

2. *Appearance. Bless their hearts, but men are ruled by the eyes. They will be more impressed with a woman—whether in a personal or professional setting—who doesn't look like something the cat dragged in. Fortunately, they're also simple creatures. They don't notice the difference between perfectly styled hair and makeup and a quick comb and coat of lipstick. Most men don't know or care whether your clothes are designer or knock-offs, just whether they are clean and ironed. Take the time to be presentable, and a man will be impressed. After all, if he "presses" his slacks in the dryer and pulls his least-smelly shirt off the floor, he thinks he's made an effort, so he doesn't expect a great deal more from you.*

3. *Demeanor. Southern men like women with soft voices and gentle manners. Now, I'm not suggesting that you have to mince around and whisper like a giggly schoolgirl, but I am saying*

that stomping around like a linebacker and yelling like his coach is not going to impress the average GRITS. Behaving like a lady will earn his respect much more than pretending to be a man.

4. *Interest. Ask him about where he comes from and who his family is. Find out his favorite sport, and then spend some time watching it with him (one hour a year should suffice). Discover why he'd want to get up before the crack of dawn to track down deer while you're still nestled in a warm bed. Find out the make and model of his first car. Remember, he might seem strong and distant, but that tough exterior is hiding a tender, sentimental heart. Take the time to show some interest in him, and he may just think you're the most fascinating woman he's ever met.*

5. *Manners. Set a good example and maybe, just maybe, he'll come around. If he's the kind of guy who is impressed by belching, chances are it isn't going to last.*

HOW TO GET A SOUTHERN MAN TO DO ANYTHING

Getting a Southern man to do just about anything for you is easy. Before those sweet little things even know what they're doing, they'll promise a lady that they'll do her taxes or fix her clogged drain. I don't manipulate men, and I don't much respect women who do. I do, however, know how to make men feel manly, which is important because a manly man will do just about anything to impress a lady.

IT'S THE GOSPEL TRUTH

"On the one hand, we'll never experience childbirth. On the other hand, we can open all our own jars."
—Bruce Willis, military brat born in West Germany

I manage to get men to help me with everything from starting my car to pruning a tree by knowing a simple fact about men: They need to feel necessary. A Southern man won't ask you to tell him how much you need him, but he is proud to help when he can. In fact, if they can't help a woman at least once a day, they're liable to run right off their rails, so take pity on them, ladies, and keep those men busy!

GETTING GRITS TO GET UP AND GO

A lot of Southern girls can get men to help them by batting their eyelashes, but the rest of us might need a little help. Follow these simple rules, and, in no time, men will be putty in your hands.

- *Tell him how much you need his help. Letting a man feel strong and capable is usually enough to get a Southern man to do anything short of wearing a tutu (and, honey, given enough motivation, he just might do that).*
- *The bigger the favor, the shorter the skirt.*
- *Let him feel that the idea of helping you is his own. It's better to tell him how worried you are about the leaves clogging your*

gutters than to ask him outright to help you clean them. If he offers to help you, he feels like he's coming to the aid of a damsel in distress. If you ask him to help you outright, he feels like he's fulfilling an obligation.

✦ Did I mention wearing a short skirt?

✦ Compliment his strengths. If he's helping you with a tune-up, tell him how much you admire his knowledge of cars. If he's helping you sort through an accounting nightmare, tell him how intelligent he is with figures. If he's helping you to clean your gutters, tell him how handy he is. It's called flattery, and it works.

✦ Some high heels with that skirt wouldn't hurt either.

✦ Don't nag. We Southern women like to talk, but, sometimes, less talk gets more results. Instead of asking him—for the fiftieth time—to take out the garbage, tell him once that you really appreciate all the help he gives you around the house. You'll find that your mother was right about catching more flies with honey than vinegar, though why on earth she wanted to catch flies at all is beyond me.

✦ High heels, a skirt, and blond hair, and he'll do just about anything.

✦ Give sincere thanks. Tell him how much you appreciate his help, and, if you can, follow up with some small help of your own. If you have a hand in the kitchen, make him his favorite dessert, or, give him another kind of sugar to sweeten his day.

HAZARDS TO AVOID

GRITS are gentle, but they'll also do whatever is necessary to protect what is dear to them. Unfortunately, those of us who've driven with Southern men know that sometimes that's a parking space. If you do see a Southern man's face reddening and his ears start smoking, apologize right away and hope you cool things down. While he'll do his best to remain a gentleman, even when he's upset, a Southern boy's anger is a thing to behold, and I don't want to be the one to do the beholding. When it comes to GRITS, it's better to avoid trouble entirely.

GOING SOUTH

My Daddy did not like the term "going South" to mean that financial times were not good. Daddy fought the phrase whenever he could. Here is a copy of a letter, which appeared on page forty-two in the "Mail Bag" of Barron's Financial Weekly *issue of April 5, 2004: "Your March 22 issue [of an otherwise credible paper],* Barron's, *twice makes a gratuitous insult to our beautiful Southland by referring to things headed in an unpleasant direction [to an unpleasant event] as heading 'South.' [The use of a region of our nation as a whipping boy with repeated slurs is indeed not an indication of good journalism.] Every time I see your use of the term 'South' to indicate something bad, it makes my blood pressure go north. Dan Coit, Chunky, Mississippi."*

The letter may not make sense to you, but it is so like my Daddy!

—Lauren Hayes,
Mississippi

Don't insult his family, including the dog, no matter how much they deserve it. Now, perhaps his cousins are a bit closer than kissing. He might have an uncle who's spent more time in the big house than his own house. Maybe his dog is smellier than the junkyard he crawled out of. No matter what old moss is clinging to the family tree, try to keep your criticisms to yourself. Though the family might be all manner of teched, it's his family, and he cares for it.

Don't insult his car or truck. Yes, I know that old junker is more rust than metal, and couldn't climb anything higher than an anthill, but it's special to him. I once knew a man who had an actual tree growing out of the bed of his truck, but he still thought that ratty old thing was his baby. Better to let your teeth rattle as you cross that little mud hole than to suggest that the ride is anything less than smooth.

Don't insult his home, even if it's on wheels. Be especially careful not to insult any "improvements" that he's made himself. You might question the need for a twenty-foot barbecue pit behind a double-wide, or why he needs a top-end hot tub when his roof is full of leaks, but he's deeply proud of the work of his hands. Southern men sometimes have their own priorities when it come to their castles; after all, how many giant satellite dishes have you seen outside of tar-paper shacks? To you, it's a dirty old firetrap, but to him, it's a gem of a home that needs nothing more than a little TLC.

Don't insult his career. He may be a janitor, a substitute teacher, or (oh, his Mama's shame) an attorney. No matter what he does, you can bet your britches that he takes pride in his job. If you feel that he could improve himself, and you honestly want to help him, it's best to do so gently. First tell him that you are impressed by the hard work and pride he takes in his job—and, if he's a Southern man, this will be honest—but that you feel he could do even better at a different job. Whatever you do, don't suggest that his job isn't worth doing. Every job is worth doing well. After all, if it weren't for sanitation workers, who'd want to walk down the streets? Be proud of him, and let him be proud of himself.

Don't suggest that Southerners are lazy, backwards, or a little slow. It might look like he's loafing on the front porch, but he may be swapping the news with his friends. It might look like he's lazing on the riverbank, but, in reality, he's watching his fishing line. It might seem that he has no pride when you look at the condition of his trailer, but just look at the new paint job and clean gutters on his Mama's house, and you'll see how he's been spending his time. It might look like he's a good old boy who's good for nothing—and, goodness, that's true of some of them, bless their hearts—but he might just be living a relaxed and civilized lifestyle.

HANDS OFF, LADIES

Southern men are generally an easygoing lot, and wouldn't speak a cross word to a lady. There are some things, however, that are off-limits, so if you want to stay on the good side of a Southern man, back off.

✦ *The gear. Also known as his fishing pole and tackle box, his guns, and his power tools. If he's a country boy, he might have a bass rig, a three-wheeler, or a pocket knife. If he's a city boy, he might have golf clubs, a tennis racket, a cell phone, or a* motorcycle. Either way, just back up and step away from the gear. Imagine how annoyed you'd be if your husband raided the bathroom and took your curling iron, then multiply that feeling by ten. I know a family of seventh-generation Southerners. Early in the 1900s, they had a gracious wooden home in Georgia, and it was threatened by fire. The house was filled with the family silver, china from England, crystal from Ireland, and even some French paintings. As the fire moved closer, the men ran frantically into the house, saving what they could. The silver melted, the china burned, the crystal burst, and the paintings became cinders. The guns, however, made it out safely, and are still in the family today.

❖ The "collection." Whether it's comic books, baseball caps, or the dreaded beer cans, it looks like garbage—but to him, it's the memories of his friends and the good times they had together. Even if he claims that those old things might be worth money some day, the real reason he keeps them is that big old sentimental heart— and he'd rather have a root canal than actually clean something up. Besides, who knows, he might be right, and that gross old Billy Beer can just might put your children through college.

❖ The grill. Even if you can't get him to boil an egg in the kitchen, when it comes time to fire up the grill, step back and let him work. The primitive part of his mind takes over, and all he can think is: fire good. Put your feet up, pour yourself a cool drink, and relax like a man.

❖ The remote. Let him flip from beach volleyball to an infomercial for a rotisserie chicken cooker and back again. He's a hunter in his heart, even if all he's catching are a few soap commercials.

✦ *The garden. He might wear a suit and tie to work, but he still sees himself as a rugged farmer providing for his family. Sure, his plantings might be no more than a few cucumbers and a tomato or two, or even just a couple of pots on the porch, but he takes as much pride in his little plot as a farmer with a couple of hundred acres. Even if you take care of the rest of the yard, leave him his little patch of ground to weed, water, and harvest. In his heart, he's a man of the earth, so let him have his fun.*

✦ *The family. Southern men know what's truly important in life. You can take away his job, his possessions, and even his home, and he'll do just fine, but he'll be lost without his family.*

CHAPTER 3

CATCHING A
SOUTHERN MAN

"There are times not to flirt. When you're sick. When you're with children. When you're on the witness stand."

—JOYCE JILLSON

"A beauty is a woman you notice. A charmer is one who notices you."

—ADLAI STEVENSON

We tease our poor GRITS, and, goodness knows, they deserve it. They're stubborn as mules, old-fashioned as slide rules, and communicative as brick walls. They're sometimes as hard to live with as those smelly old dawgs they love so much. I've married four of them, so, goodness gracious, I'm aware that GRITS aren't always easy to handle.

Nonetheless, with all of his problems, we want nothing better than to catch a Southern man for ourselves, and to help the women we love do the same. Since we want Southern men, and Southern men want us, it seems like finding a Southern mate would be easy. But love is hard, even for incurably romantic Southerners. Isn't it true the Southern man that you're after never seems interested in you, and vice versa? Simple timing matters a lot in love. There's a lot of fish in the lake, and a lot of them are big old suckers. You'll have to throw a few of the bad ones back to get to that prize bass. Once you find the perfect Southern man, you've got to show him that you're the perfect Southern woman, and that's not always easy in a world where true ladies (those who would nevah, evah, chew gum) are often as scarce as gentlemen.

THE HUNT

"THE RULES" OF FINDING
A SOUTHERN MAN

Some writers give advice that women should follow certain "rules," including waiting more than one day to return calls and staying aloof, if not acting downright rude. Whoever made up these "rules" was not a Southern lady. Ladies behave like ladies, even when they're on the lookout for a man. If he's a gentleman, he'll be happy to have a woman in his life who behaves with common decency. If he responds better to "rules" and mind games, he isn't a man that you'd want in your life anyway.

- ✦ *Ladies treat everyone—eligible bachelors included—with respect. He may be as alluring as roadkill, but you still need to take the time to tell him no. If a man calls you, you should call him back as soon as possible, even if that call is just to let him down gently.*
- ✦ *When you converse with him, be polite and interested. Your eyes may glaze over as he discusses the foreign tax credit or the two dozen cute things his toddler said that morning, but yawning openly and looking around the room for an exit is just not the Southern way. The best "rule" to follow is the Golden Rule: Treat a man like you would want to be treated.*
- ✦ *As much as possible, be open and honest with the men in your life. No, you don't have to point out that his toupee looks like a dying squirrel, at least until you know him better, but you should never lie or tell half-truths. Don't tell them that you're busy when all you're doing is painting your toenails and watching* American Idol.

✦ *Appearance is important to a man, but it shouldn't be all that he notices about you. Watch those neck- and hemlines. Many young women today walk around in public with their lingerie on the outside, and when I see that, I blush for their poor mothers.*

✦ *Stay on the lookout for interested men, but don't let your hunt be the most important part of your life. Cultivate your own interests, whether those interests involve work, church, volunteering, or hobbies, so that you can find happiness and contentment with or without a man. The more interesting your life is, the more interesting you will be. Like us, men want people in their lives who find joy in living.*

✦ *Men are just as nervous about dating us as we are about dating them. Southern men are charming creatures, and that charm can hide the nervous feelings they have around us. When you talk to a man, be polite, smile, and ask him about himself. Your kindness and interest in him will set him at ease. Once he's relaxed and happy, he'll notice the wonderful GRITS who made him feel that way.*

✦ *Even when we reach the shady side of fifty, Southern girls still want to date men that their mothers would be proud of. If you're a mother, teach your boy to treat women with respect and kindness. If you're dating, don't stay with a man who treats you as less than a lady. Now, not all men, even Southern men, I'm sad to say, learned to open doors for ladies, so don't throw a man over for a detail like that. Do, however, demand that a man treat you with kindness and respect you as a woman. You are a Southern woman, honey, and you deserve the best.*

If you're a single Southern woman, you're in luck . . . finding and dating a Southern man is about as much fun as you can have without breaking the Ten Commandments. Southern gentlemen are everywhere, but you're more likely to find one if you look in gentlemanly places. Bars and clubs are fine for hanging out with the girls, but if you're looking for a life partner, well, ask yourself whether you want to spend the rest of your life with the man who leers at you after pounding back three Harvey Wallbangers. Go to places where you wouldn't be ashamed to be seen by your mama, and you'll be more likely to find a man worth having.

IT'S THE GOSPEL TRUTH

If you are looking for a Southern man, buy a big dog such as a boxer or a mastiff. If you're a man looking for a Southern woman, try walking around with a baby (though, heavens, I sure hope you don't try to buy one!).

If you want to help your friend snag a man, remember, the best way to find a man is to put yourself in a situation where you see plenty of them. Ask your friend out often, and when you go, visit places where you'll see men. Precious little tearooms and cute little boutiques are all well and good for female bonding, but for ladies on the prowl, sporting events, country clubs, and church socials make a bit more sense. If she's shy, don't be afraid to walk up to a man yourself. Ask the good-looking man in the hardware store if he can give you—

and your friend, of course—tips on fixing her tiles, and, pretty soon, the two of them just might be doing their grouting together. If you want to help your daughter, it's best just to step back and let nature take its course. After all, no girl wants to date a man her mother set her up with.

IF YOU WANT A GENTLEMAN, DON'T GO TO A "GENTLEMAN'S CLUB!" WHERE TO FIND SOUTHERN GENTLEMEN

✦ *Places of worship: He's visiting God's house, so he must be acquainted with the owner.*

✦ *Sports clubs: Energetic and successful men often exercise in the morning. If you can pry yourself out of bed, you'll meet men who are in shape and ready to go for the day ahead. Even if you don't meet anyone, you'll soon become more fit, and have the energy you need to continue the hunt.*

✦ *Classes: Lessons in golf, tennis, scuba diving, wine appreciation, foreign languages, finance, and even shooting are great places to meet men who are interested in something other than beer and television.*

✦ *Grocery store: Everybody has to eat. The best time to shop is early evening, right after work. Keep in mind that what he has in his cart can give you clues to his character: If he has nothing but cheap beer and sugary children's cereal, avoid him. Single men often have carts full of single-serving frozen dinners, but these* days many eligible men are cooking well for themselves, so don't avoid the man with the arugula, fine wine, and filet mignon. Honey, if he's single, Southern, and can cook, you've hit the jackpot.

✦ Coffee shop: Frequent trips to your local gourmet coffee shop will not only keep you energized, they're great places to meet single men. Sit awhile with a paper, but remember to peek over it every once in a while to see who has a taste for java (or Southern ladies!).

✦ Volunteer: Volunteering for something you care about let's you do something good while looking for Mr. Right.

✦ "Manly" shows: Car, boat, gun, and knife shows attract men like watermelon rinds attract hogs, with just about as much grunting and slobbering. Men will be excited to see a woman who shares their interests. Just don't stand 'tween them and that new concept car; you'll risk ruining your hairdo, or worse, as the men trample past you.

✦ Friends: Pride has no place in the hunt for a man. Don't be ashamed to ask your friends to keep their eyes open for eligible men. It's not a good idea to date at your office, but their office is fair game.

GETTING HIS ATTENTION

Everyone who's lived with a Southern man knows that sometimes to get his attention, you need to come near to slapping him upside the head. Southern men are sweet as can be, but sometimes they sure can be clueless. To get a Southern man's attention, you will often need to put yourself forward.

Now, I'm not suggesting that you act anything but lady-like. In fact, being aggressive or bawdy will turn off most men, Southern or not. I am saying that you need to smile more, talk more, and just plain put yourself out where men can see you. Staring off into space, looking distant and moody, may work if you're in a fashion magazine (or just look like you belong in one), but most women who do so just look cranky and unapproachable. I'm not against asking a man out rather than waiting for him to ask you; at the worst, he'll say no, but more likely he'll be flattered by the attention and say yes right away.

Some women believe that they can't make hearts flutter anymore just because most men in their age group have pacemakers. I say a few years just make a Southern belle ring all the sweeter. You don't have to be in your twenties, or even your thirties, forties, or fifties, to make the man in your life feel like a schoolboy. It's true that the quickest way to a man's heart is through his eyes, but you don't have to be a supermodel to attract a Southern man (and just because you have a few years doesn't mean you can't still be a heartbreaker!). In fact, though stiletto heels and microminis may attract a lot of men quickly, those men aren't likely to be the kind of GRITS who stay around. Southern men want to settle down with a girl who is kind, gentle, and raised right. They want a woman who is presentable, down-to-earth, and confident. You may spend thousands of dollars on Prada, but a Southern man prefers a woman in a T-shirt and tight jeans any day, so long as her head, and her heart, are in the right place.

Whatever your appearance, there is a Southern man out there who is right for you. And I can't say it enough: You don't have to be rail-thin or model-pretty to find a Southern man. Physical appearance may be the first thing that many men notice, but it isn't the last; a woman who is pretty inside is much more likely to keep the interest of a GRITS after the first glance. Focus on your inner beauty if you are interested in winning a man for a lifetime.

BEATS ALL I HAVE EVER SEEN!

Although many women believe that you cannot be too rich or too thin, studies show that they may be wrong. When asked to rate the body shape that men prefer, female participants in the studies consistently believed that males preferred a thinner body type than they actually did. To men, a bit of body fat means there's just a bit more of you to cuddle!

BUILDING A SOUTHERN BELLE ATTITUDE

Exuding an air of confidence, poise, and calm will draw men like flies to honey. Here's some tips on how to do it.

✦ *Change that voice in your head. Be positive. Encourage and praise yourself. Southern women are taught to be self-effacing and demure, and those qualities are admirable, but it's also important to know your own value. Don't be arrogant or boastful, but do feel happy with who you are.*

✦ *At the first sign of negative thoughts, stop yourself, and try to think of something positive. If thinking alone isn't enough, it's often helpful to sit down and write things about yourself that are good, valuable, and worthy.*

✦ *Call a true friend and discuss your feelings. She may offer feedback on how to change yourself, but, chances are, she'll tell you all those wonderful things about yourself that you, being modest, overlooked.*

✦ *Stand straight and walk tall. There's a reason debutantes had to spend hours walking with books atop their heads, honey!*

✦ *Even if you don't feel confident, try to act confident. Once you get into the habit of appearing self-assured, you'll find that the real thing comes naturally.*

✦ *Every evening, look in the mirror and tell yourself that you're beautiful. Trust me, even if the years have given you a few crow's-feet, too much chocolate cake has given you an extra chin, nature has given you thin lips, and your children have given you gray hairs, there's something beautiful in every face. My sister, Mavis, always says (only to herself in front of mirrors, of course): "You good-looking woman. Don't you ever die!" With this attitude, she's never been without a man.*

There are all sorts of Southern men out there, with all sorts of tastes in women. Sure, they all want someone who behaves like a lady, but remember that you can be a lady in a country-and-western bar just as easily as you can be a lady in a country club. Whether you're light or dark, thin or heavy, a little bit country or a little bit rock-and-roll, there's a man out there for you. Keep hunting, and you'll find that the perfect man will soon be in your sights.

MATCHMAKER

Going out to find a man can be fun, but some of us are too shy, or just too darned busy. When you let your friends serve as matchmaker, you'll have dozens of eyes looking for the perfect man, not just two. Any Southern man will tell you that a Southern woman just can't help trying to bring young lovers together. In fact, if you're single and Southern, you may find yourself wanting to get married just to avoid all the matchmaking!

SURVIVING THE BLIND DATE

- *Even if he shows up in black socks and sandals, give him a chance. Your friends must have felt that there was something to see in him, so try to find out what it is. Maybe he's a diamond in the rough, and he needs a Southern girl's touch to make him shine.*
- *Avoid a Saturday night date. A cup of coffee or a quick walk in the park puts less pressure on both of you. If he's a catch, you can meet for dinner and a movie some other time—don't be afraid to say yes to a spur-of-the moment invitation—and if he's not, you can throw him back after only a half hour.*
- *If you can, try to meet him for the first time as part of a group. You'll both be more comfortable around mutual friends, and you can always meet your girlfriends in the ladies' room for gossip and advice.*
- *Even if he's a dud, thank your friend for trying. We don't all have the same tastes or standards, and she was just trying to help you.*
- *If he's really, truly awful, just remember the details so that you can laugh about it for the rest of your life.*

ART OF FLIRTING

Flirting is like breathing to Southern men and women; it's just a natural part of life. Just because it's natural, though, doesn't mean that we can't use a bit of practice.

Flirting is an art. And like any art, it requires practice. Even though they have talent, Mary Lou Retton couldn't do a backflip until she'd fallen a few times, and LeAnn Rimes couldn't sing until she'd hit a few flat notes. All great artists, including flirters, had to fall down a few times to learn; just because you are seeing them at their best doesn't mean that they didn't look like gangly, awkward fools when they started. You'll look and feel mighty silly flirting before you get practice, so be prepared for a man to ask you if you have a speck of dust in your eye as you attempt to bat your lashes at him. Don't be afraid to fail once, twice, or twenty times; everything worth doing is difficult, after all.

 IT'S THE GOSPEL TRUTH

"Yeah, I flirt. I'm not blind and I'm not dead!"
—*Dolly Parton, Tennessee*

You don't have to be a stunning belle to flirt. In fact, some of the best and most famous flirters have been rather plain. The secret to flirting is making the other person feel more like a man or a woman. Making any person feel more interesting and more wanted will make them more interested in you. It

spark alive. Flirting with a friend or stranger can make you feel like the sweet, seductive woman you undoubtedly are. Now, I know I don't have to tell a Southern woman that, if you're attached, you should never go beyond sweet words and a flutter of the eyelashes, but a giggle with a stranger can help remind you that you're a desirable woman, and bringing that feeling to your relationship can make you a better wife or girlfriend.

CHAPTER 4

THE DATING GAME

"Computer dating is fine. If you're a computer."

—RITA MAE BROWN, VIRGINIA

"You have to kiss a lot of toads before you find a handsome prince."

—ANONYMOUS

Once you meet a Southern man, there's a chance that you might want to have him around for a while. Winning a man over usually involves dating. Don't be afraid of dating; try to look at it like marriage without all of the work. He'll open the door for you, talk and charm you through the evening, but at the end of the night, you don't have to pick his laundry up off the floor. If he takes you to a fancy restaurant, you don't have to worry about facing next month's credit card bill.

While dating, a Southern man is on his best behavior. After you're married or living together, he'll discover the joys of sitting shirtless in front of the television, watching a sport he's never even heard of before, and eating potato chips off his rapidly expanding midsection. Dating can be awkward and heartbreaking, but it's also a Southern man's golden hour, so enjoy it while you can.

ONE ON ONE

Flirting is a lot of fun, but if you hope to progress further with a Southern man, you're going to have to date him one on one. First impressions are important, so do what you can to please his optic nerve. After all, you expect him to arrive with his hair neatly combed and wearing his best pressed (or, at a minimum, least dirty) pants. You should show him the same courtesy. When you're choosing your clothes, remember to be feminine, but don't go overboard. Wear fitted, flattering clothes, preferably a skirt or a dress (with a hemline that wouldn't embarrass your Mama!). Have your makeup, mascara, and hair in place, but keep it gentle and understated. Men love perfume, even if they don't consciously realize that they're noticing it, but keep the fragrance subtle. Every woman looks better in heels, but they should be of a tasteful height. Most important, be comfortable, be confident, and be ready to have a good time.

DOWN-HOME DICTIONARY

courtship ['kȯrt 'ship] n. *The practice, increasingly popular, of getting to know potential marriage partners in a family, community, and church-centered context. No groping in the back row of dark movie theaters, no sneaking into the girls' dormitory after hours, just good, clean fun.*

A Southern man will behave like a gentleman on the date. A classic Southern gentleman will walk you to the car and open the door. He'll pull out your chair at dinner. He'll smile and compliment you. Now, these days, I'm afraid to say that a lot of young men, even Southern men, don't know how to escort a lady on the town. I don't have to tell a Southern lady that it's a parent's responsibility to teach a boy to treat a woman properly. It's best if he sees his father being chivalrous toward his mother, but if not, a mother should sit a son down and tell him it's about time he started behaving better than the old man.

Opening the door is something we can live without— reluctantly. But we can't live without respect. A man should always behave as if you are a fine Southern lady; cussing, drinking too much, fighting, cussing and fighting while drinking, and asking for anything more than a kiss on the first date are not the Southern way (or at least not the ways we want to uphold). If he doesn't respect you as a lady, there's nothing wrong with opening the door yourself . . . then shutting it right in his face.

OPENING THE DOOR
FOR LAURIE

My first lesson on dating women came when I was nine or ten years old and living in Decatur, Georgia. The Youth Director at our church announced that we were going to have a bonfire. We were told we could bring a friend, and the parents were assured that there would be plenty of chaperones just in case any of the boys decided to bring a friend of the female gender. We were careful not to say "girlfriend" because, at that age, a lot of us didn't have our cootie shots yet.

I decided to ask "a friend of mine, who is a girl" who lived two doors down. I asked Laurie, and she agreed, but only after getting permission from both our mothers. The evening of the bonfire, I went running to the door, shouting, "Mama, I'm going to get Laurie!" I was baffled when me mother said that we needed to pick her up instead; she lived two doors down! Nevertheless, I waited.

Well, we got into the car and drove down two driveways. My mother told me to get Laurie, and when I rolled down the window to shout for her, my mother interrupted: "Gerald, go to the door and get her." "Why can't you just blow the horn?" I asked. "Gerald, go to the door and get Laurie!" she said firmly. With a quick, "Yes, Ma'am," I went to the door.

I was one bewildered boy walking up the door. When I got there, Laurie's mother opened it. I asked if she was ready, and when her mother said yes, I headed back to the car. My mother sent me marching back. I had to ask Laurie if she was ready. By this point, I was completely dumbfounded. This was just Laurie, after all. I asked Laurie if she was ready, and she replied that she was.

With relief, I started for the car again, only to hear my mother say, "Gerald, wait and walk her to the car and open the door for her." At this point, I thought we'd never get out of that driveway. I never realized how complex it was to take a girl (who is a friend) to a bonfire.

When we got back that evening, my mother had more instructions. I had to get out, go around, open the car door, walk her to her front door, and make sure she got in before we left. I followed instructions, and as we stood at the door, I asked Laurie: "Is this where we kiss now?"

The door opened quickly, and Laurie's mother replied. "Not this *time! Laurie, tell Gerald good night." I still follow the lessons I learned that night. I open and shut doors for all women, especially my wife, who, incidentally, is named Laurie! After all I went through that night, though, I still think I deserved that kiss.*

—Gerald L. Cooper,
Georgia

Once you're on the date, remember that it isn't about how much money he spends; it's about how you feel together. I have had more fun dining out on a hot dog at a ball game than I've had at a fancy restaurant. As much as I love being made a fuss over, I hate to think that a man of limited means is stretching himself just to be with me. Taking the time to show genuine interest is more attractive to a woman than maxing out a credit card. Believe me, I've had roses and champagne, and I've had carnations and Coca-Cola, and both are wonderful if there's a courteous, attentive Southern gentleman standing there holding them for me.

If a man has worked up the courage to ask you out, you should give him the courtesy of your undivided attention. He wants to get to know you, but it's important that you take the time to get to know him. Ask him about himself, and really listen to his answers. A Southern man won't tell you everything at first; we Southerners like to hold back and enjoy the long process of getting to know each other. It just wouldn't be fun if we told our life stories on the first date! Focus on what he does reveal; I've discovered that if you really listen, you'll get to know the real man more quickly.

MAKING A DATE FUN
UNTIL DESSERT . . .
OR AFTER, SUGAR!

✦ *Never bring up religion, politics, or barbecue (you'll never get Southerners to agree on these).*

✦ *Don't be afraid to do something corny or old-fashioned: bowling, minature golf, and county fairs can be lots of fun, especially if he's mystified by any conversation not involving baseball stats.*

✦ *Remember his name! First, last, and, preferably, middle.*

✦ *Never, ever talk about exes, yours or his.*

✦ *Never, ever ask for a doggy bag.*

✦ *Bring a small toothbrush, and slip into the restroom after dinner to use it. Nothing spoils your sweet Southern smile faster than onion breath.*

IT'S THE GOSPEL TRUTH

When you're dating after a divorce or widowhood, you might be as nervous as a schoolgirl at her first homecoming dance. Don't be afraid to admit your fears to your date, just be sure to mention your nervousness once, and then never do it again. A Southern man will be sensitive to your fears, but nobody has a good time when he knows that his date is across the table quaking in her boots.

MY SOUTHERN GENTLEMAN

I had just moved to Florida from North Carolina and was working in the office of the trucking company where Buddy worked. It was not love at first sight, even though he was gorgeous. Buddy asked me out five times before I said yes. I wasn't playing hard to get. I just didn't want to go out with him. I didn't want to rush into anything just because I was new in town.

Our first date was on Valentine's Day. He planned to cook dinner for me. Then we would go see the movie Love Story with Ryan O'Neal and Ali MacGraw. Sounds like a nice evening, right?

The spaghetti dinner he was preparing for me went down the drain . . . literally! As he was draining the noodles, his hand slipped, and half the pasta slid down the drain. He had to leave me alone in his apartment, which was absolutely spotless and so well organized, while he rushed to the store for more noodles. While the noodles were cooking, he surprised me with a Baby Ruth candy bar. He had taken the time to find out they are my favorite.

After dinner, we went to the movie, and in the lobby of the theater, he dropped the bucket of popcorn. This evening was getting worse, not better! Finally, at my front door, I expected a good-night kiss, or at least an attempt, but all I got was a handshake.

Staying true to the attributes of a Southern gentleman, over the next few weeks the most serious, romantic gesture displayed by Buddy was to hold my hand. It was a month before he attempted to kiss me, but I began to receive flowers at work every Wednesday. I was the envy of every woman working there. The kiss finally came and I fell in love. It was everything I had anticipated! We married and had three wonderful children and now have five grandchildren. After thirty-three years of marriage, he still sends flowers with Baby Ruth candy bars.

It hasn't been easy. No marriage ever is, but ours in particular because Buddy suffers from post-traumatic stress disorder from his three tours of duty in Vietnam and the horrors he endured during that war. Our marriage was not supposed to last, according to Vietnam veteran statistics. But, together, we raised a family, and today, still together, we pray for our son who is currently serving his second deployment to Iraq.

Despite all the trials and tribulations, my wish is that my children will find mates that have even a fraction of the character of their father. You've heard the expression "they broke the mold when they made him"; well, that is my Buddy.

—Linda L. McLelland,
North Carolina

WHAT SOUTHERN MEN LOVE TO HEAR ON A DATE

+ I don't like to wear much makeup. It never takes me long to get ready.
+ I love cubic zirconia—just make sure it's big!
+ Please pass the mashed potatoes, and, I declare, I'd love some of that gravy, too!
+ Why don't we stay home and I'll grill you something?
+ I love it when a man goes on a trip with his guy friends. Goodness, I'll even make the reservations.
+ I have season tickets!

IS HE A GENTLEMAN?

IT'S THE GOSPEL TRUTH

I recently went on a date with a man who told me that his marriage had ended because he had an affair with a thirty-year-old who looked eighteen. He went on to say that she lives with a doctor, but she's not married to him; he sees her only occasionally! Obviously, I never dated this man again. Most men aren't that blatant, but when he speaks about other women, pay attention to what he says, because he is going to treat you the same way.

IS HE A KEEPER
OR A PLAYER?

A keeper:

→ *respects himself by taking care of himself physically, emotionally, and spiritually.*

→ *respects his family, friends, and neighbors.*

→ *gives back to his community and helps others.*

→ *calls you to tell you if he is going to be early or late.*

→ *means what he says and says what he means.*

→ *listens to you when you talk.*

→ *shows interest in your children and/or your pets.*

→ *does a good job at work, no matter what his title or status might be, and is a loyal and dependable employee.*

→ *is attentive to you when he's with you, not to his cell phone or the attractive woman at the next table.*

A player:

* *doesn't take care of himself, or takes care of himself only because of vanity, which means he looks in the mirror more than you do.*
* *thinks: "Family? What's that?"*
* *thinks: "Volunteering? I guess it's a good way to meet some cute candy stripers."*
* *is chronically late without a good excuse, or encounters a suspicious amount of bad traffic on the way to your house.*
* *says: "I said that? I must have been drinking."*
* *says: "So, enough about you . . . I've got a great story."*
* *says: "Children? Oh, don't call me; I'll call you."*
* *brags about accomplishments or (good heavens!) tells you his salary.*
* *remarks about the attractiveness of other women while he's with you, or, even worse, asks another woman for her number.*

It's a lot more important to me that a man shares my values and my interests than that he has an important job and a lot of money. A man who rakes leaves or cleans pipes, but who is gentle, chivalrous, and honest, is much more of a gentleman than a surgeon or an executive who thinks that he's God's gift to a woman (or more than one woman at a time). I've had people offer to set me up on dates and tell me that I'll like the man . . . he's rich. While I can't think of anyone who'd rather be poor than rich, I'd trade the fancy cars and large bank accounts for a man who is truly a gentleman. What makes GRITS special is not money or status; it's that they know how to treat a Southern woman like a lady, and make every woman, whether she's wearing real diamonds or paste from the five-and-dime, feel like a princess.

I tease GRITS, but there are plenty of good ones out there. Don't let the slobbering of a few dogs scare you away from the real men. Keep trying, and a good one will come along. I've been married four times, but I still believe that the right man is out there for me somewhere. If I have hope, honey, anyone can, so keep your eyes open and a smile on your face, and your prince will come along.

KEEPING HIM COMING BACK FOR MORE

If you've found a true Southern gentleman, goodness gracious, don't let him go. And if you have an extra, honey, give me a call! It seems like GRITS are getting harder to catch, so if you're lucky enough to reel one in, hold on tight, no matter how slippery he might be!

It's important that you do what you can to deepen your relationship, and to keep it alive. A Southern man isn't going to be impressed with shallow things—at least not for long enough to build a relationship—so, honey, don't get that permanent eyeliner or that liposuction. If it makes you feel better, fine, but don't do it for him. Take care of your outside, of course, but it's more important to take care of what's inside. A Southern man will be impressed with a woman who proves to be honest, loving, and down-to-earth. There aren't any short-

cuts or quick tips on making a relationship deep and lasting.
What he wants in a serious relationship is the same thing that
a Southern woman wants: someone who loves him, who cher-
ishes him, who makes him feel special.

SIX WAYS TO LOVE YOUR GRITS-AND-GRAVY MAN!

1. *When he does something special for you, tuck a thank-you note into his pocket or briefcase.*
2. *Give him a foot massage.*
3. *Bring him a glass of his favorite drink while he's watching television, reading, or relaxing.*
4. *When you know that he's had a hard week, surprise him with a freshly washed car, mown grass, or shined shoes.*
5. *Send him flowers (if he is the kind of man who won't think that's sissy!), or buy him tickets to a game.*
6. *Make him a hot chicken dinner . . . and let him have the white meat.*

IT'S THE GOSPEL TRUTH

Never lie—not even a white lie—to a Southern man. If you make a mistake, don't make excuses. Fess up and tell him you did wrong; he may be upset at first, but he'll be impressed that you are trustworthy, and, ultimately, your relationship will deepen.

A Southern man, like a Southern woman, is modest enough never to brag of himself . . . that's your job, honey! He may look at his toes or even blush (what a sweet sight on a tough, manly face!), but, trust me, he appreciates your sincere compliments. I'm not saying to intentionally make him feel uncomfortable or, even worse, to embellish the truth. I'm just saying to let your man know how proud you are of him, and how much he means to you. A specific, meaningful compliment is the best kind: "It's really sweet how you take time for your mother"; "I love to watch you play softball—you sure like fine in those uniform pants"; or "I'm impressed with your beautiful garden and the care that you take to make it special." Being fawning and fake will drive a GRITS away, but taking the time to tell him that what he does matters, and that someone notices, will make him feel proud.

IT'S THE GOSPEL TRUTH

A Southern man would never allow a lady to take care of the meal . . . so surprise him! Take care of the check ahead of time, and don't forget to tell him to add a generous tip.

BEING DATABLE ON THE FIRST, OR THE FIFTIETH, DATE

❖ As we grow comfortable, it's natural to start slacking off, and give in to the temptation to throw on some sweatpants and pull back your hair in a ponytail. You don't have to wear your diamonds every date—though why not, honey?—but you should always be lovely.

❖ Don't try to compete with the other women in his life. His mother, his daughter, and even his dog are important to him, and the competition will hurt him (and you). Even if he chooses you over them, you will never really win.

❖ Be sincerely interested in him, and if you aren't, ask yourself why you're with him.

❖ Listen, and encourage him to talk about himself by asking thoughtful questions. Don't nag or interrogate, but do ask about the big project at work, the book he's reading, or the big game.

❖ If a man is spending time at your house, keep high-quality, soft sheets on your bed, surprise him after a shower with a warm towel, and welcome him home with a hot bubble bath.

❖ Be realistic. No one, not even a Southern man, is perfect. Forgive, and then forget, for now and forever, his mistakes.

SOUTHERN MEN "KNEAD" TOUCH

We all love and need to be touched, and Southerners especially appreciate a loving hand. We welcome a hand on the shoulder or the arm while we talk, a hug and a kiss to welcome an old friend, and a pat on the back when we do well.

Massage provides closeness and healing, and it allows you to truly connect with the person you are touching. Best of all, it allows you physical intimacy without doing anything that you, or your Mama, would be ashamed of. Here are some tips:

✦ Remove all jewelry, and make sure that your nails are trimmed and free of snags (ouch!).

✦ Set the mood with a warm room, light music, low lighting, a comfortable place to lie down, and warm oils or lotions (always put lotion in the palm of your hand to warm it before applying).

✦ Observe his posture before you begin. Many people concentrate their tension in one part of the body. If he grinds his jaw, focus on his head, face, and neck. If he holds his shoulders tight, focus on the shoulders and upper back. If he clenches his hands, hand massage may make him feel better.

✦ Keep at least one hand on him at all times.

✦ Your touch should be firm and steady, but don't go overboard and try to manhandle the muscles. If he shows any discomfort, ease up.

✦ Simple but effective touches include: gently kneading his neck, running your hands with firm pressure on both sides of the spine, *using the thumbs or balls of the hands to rub out knots, and massaging the neck in gentle circles.*

✦ *You don't have to be an expert or have expert moves; he'll appreciate the touch and intimacy. Relax and have fun.*

CHAPTER 5

ROPING HIM IN

"I married the first man I ever kissed. When I tell this to my children, they just about throw up."

—FORMER FIRST LADY BARBARA BUSH

"The dedicated life is the life worth living. You must give with your whole heart."

—ANNIE DILLARD

ost Southern women want to be happily married to a Southern man. No matter what her age, a Southern woman will not give up looking, and there've been plenty of blushing brides who've seen more than their share of Junes. Southern men want to settle down too, though they may take their sweet time doing it. Whether it's your first (and, I hope, last) marriage, or your fifth, if you're Southern, it's a time of hope, of excitement, and of love.

MEETING HIS FAMILY

A Southern man is going to want you to meet those near and dear to him before he decides to make you part of his family. He won't necessarily push you away just because Mama or his kids don't like your looks at first—if he did, there wouldn't be very many marriages in the South!—but he will consider how well you get along with his family.

You may be nervous when you meet them, but the best you can do is to be yourself. He loves you, so they should, too. Dress conservatively, keep a smile on your face, and have a kind word for everyone—even that quiet cousin who spends the evening staring into space and picking his teeth. Don't talk about anything controversial, and if they bring up religion or politics, try to keep your nose out of it. After all, it's better to be remembered as that quiet and polite woman that their boy brought home than the one who preached her fiery opinions about heaven and hell (and which one his family is bound for).

HOW TO CHARM HIS CHILDREN

* *Remember their ages, and act appropriately. If you want to make an enemy for life, give a thirteen-year-old girl a Barbie doll.*
* *Imagine how you'd feel if you stumbled into the kitchen for your morning Cheerios, and a stranger was sitting at the table in your father's robe. Let the father introduce you into their lives gradually, first with a casual dinner or night watching television, then, slowly, let your relationship grow.*
* *Treat their father with love and respect.*
* *You're not Mama, so don't try to take her place. Whatever you do, don't say a bad word about her.*
* *Don't try to bribe them. It might seem like the easiest thing now to buy them video games and sugary treats, but if you expect to be in their father's life long-term, is that the precedent that you want to set? It's a bit of software today, but in a couple of years, it will be a new computer with all the bells and whistles.*
* *Let Daddy discipline them, and when it comes time for you to take a greater role in their lives, let him explain to them that they have to accept your authority.*

IT'S THE GOSPEL TRUTH

Don't expect his children, whether young or fully grown, to accept you right away. In fact, you should expect to be treated like the wicked witch come to steal away Daddy. You can and should demand that they treat you with a modicum of politeness, but give them some space to resent you. Time, kindness, and smiles will bring even his sulky teenage children around.

Sit down with your husband and write down the dates of birthdays and anniversaries for every member of his family, or as many as he can remember—he is a man, after all! If he doesn't have all the dates handy, go ahead and ask your mother-in-law; she just might appreciate your effort. Send a hand-written note on special days to let your new family know that you are thinking of them. An expensive gift is not necessary; you'll win more hearts will a few special words than with tennis bracelets and fine Kentucky bourbon.

While any family member is difficult to meet, it's the mother-in-law that strikes true fear in the heart of a Southern girl. A Southern woman can face unemployment, cancer, or a lawsuit and still stay calm and cool. After all, we Southerners have seen trouble, and we've always been able to come through with our heads held high. Facing a mother-in-law, on the other hand, can turn the strongest Southern woman weak in the knees. Maybe it's because we want so desperately for her to like us. Or maybe she really is the monster hiding under the bed, and you can be sure that there's not a woman in the world who can please her.

IT'S THE GOSPEL TRUTH

"Mama and Daddy King represent the best in manhood and womanhood, the best in a marriage, the kind of people we are trying to become."

—*Coretta Scott King, wife of Dr. Martin Luther King, Jr., and a daughter-in-law any parent would love, Georgia*

Believe it or not, it's possible for a Southern women to dearly love, or at least get along with, her mother-in-law. Sure, she may offer one too many helpful tips on improving your meatloaf or getting a bit more exercise for those full hips, but she's also given you the man you love. If you can be grateful to her for the wonderful man that she's given the world, that emotion will shine through in your face and attitude, and she'll sense your goodwill. She isn't a bogeyman, after all, but a bogeywoman, twice as scary but only half as bad. If she's hard to love at first, it's probably that her girdle is a little bit too tight, or maybe she's just an overprotective mom.

IT'S THE GOSPEL TRUTH

"Humor is always based on a modicum of truth. Have you ever heard a joke about a father-in-law?"
—*Dick Clark, New York*
   (*sound like he needs a Southern mother-in-law to me!*)

HOW TO CHARM HIS MAMA

❖ *Tell her he looks just like her. Don't worry—even if he looks like Don King on a bad hair day, she thinks he's the most beautiful thing in the world.*

❖ *Remind her that behind every successful man is his Mama.*

❖ *Thank her as often as possible for raising such a fine Southern man.*

❖ *Name your first daughter after her—and just maybe the baby will inherit the pearls!*

❖ *Take his name, even if it's Hogg or Nutt.*

❖ *Always ask about her Mama.*

❖ *Tell her how much she means to her son, and suggest to both of them that he treat her to a special weekend . . . without you getting in the way.*

❖ *Make sure she feels like she's the favorite guest in your home. Go ahead, break out the good towels.*

❖ *Be yourself!*

Part of getting along with your mother-in-law is to really listen to, and honor, what she's saying. I was getting my hair done at the beauty parlor—as everyone in the South knows, it's the best source of wit and wisdom—and a woman told me a story about her mother-in-law. For fifteen years, her mother-in-law didn't like her, and the poor woman could never figure out why. Her mother-in-law occasionally made comments about the condition of her husband's shirts, but the woman didn't really listen to what she was saying. Finally, she put two and two together, and she realized that her mother-in-law disliked her because of a little ironing! She asked her mother-in-law to help her with the shirts, and, overnight, the two became friends. Now, I'm not suggesting that all problems with mother-in-laws are this easy to solve, or, goodness, that your average Southern mother-in-law would dislike her son's wife because of a few wrinkles, but I am saying that listening to her can help your relationship.

She may not always tell you so, but your mother-in-law will appreciate any good woman who makes her little boy happy. Don't be afraid of meeting a prospective mother-in-law; keep a smile on your face, and love in your heart, and she'll come around to you. If you haven't always seen eye to eye, keep trying. She knows your husband's faults, sometimes better than you do, and you both love him anyway. Whatever faults she sees in you, she'll grow to love you as well. If she never does come around, well, it's best to put up with her for the sake of your husband (and, later, your children).

If you do not live in the same city as your mother-in-law, she may feel cut off from her son's and her grandchildren's lives. As much as they love their mothers, sometimes Southern boys are a little reluctant to reach out to her across the miles, so become her favorite daughter-in-law by stepping up! Next Christmas, give her an empty photo album. At the end of each month, send her a page full of your pictures. At the end of the year, she'll have a year's worth of memories, and she'll know that your family was thinking of her every moment.

It's possible to stay friends with your husband's family even if your own marriage doesn't survive. I myself try to maintain friendships with my "ex" families. In fact, my mother-in-law, Sibyle, was one of my best friends. Before and after my divorce, she helped me raise my two daughters and left them with many wonderful memories of her. In fact, we were so close that I came to her for advice about my subsequent relationships with men.

For the sake of the children, if no one else, it's important to keep relations as happy as possible. I know a woman who arranged for her ex-mother-in-law to buy a house two doors down from hers, even though she and her ex-husband had been divorced for almost twenty years. Like father, like son, both men in their lives had strayed from their marriages and cheated on their spouses. When the marriage broke up, the mother-in-law sympathized, and the two women became, and remain, good friends.

IT'S THE GOSPEL TRUTH

"Hey Roseanne, I just saw all the animals in the neighborhood running in circles, so I guess that means your mother is arriving soon."
—John Goodman as Dan Conner, *Roseanne*

FATHER-IN-LAW KNOWS BEST

Everyone complains about her mother-in-law, but a lot less is said about the father-in-law. Sometimes, a father-in-law can truly be a problem, but most Southern fathers-in-law are just big old softies that want to share a laugh and a bowl of banana pudding.

✦ *If he doesn't look up from his game to acknowledge your presence when entering a room, don't take it personally. After all, no matter how beautiful you might be, there's nothing that you can do to compete with Dale Earnhardt, Jr.*

✦ *Southern fathers are simple. Most just want a comfortable chair, a good meal, and laughing grandchildren. Learn to bake his favorite dish, and stay out of that favorite chair, and you're as good as Mother Teresa in his book.*

✦ *Some fathers-in-law just can't wait to share a story with you; the mother-in-law has heard everything he has to say ten times, and his buddies have tales of their own to share. Just taking the time to listen to his story about Cousin Zeke falling off the roof can make you the favorite daughter-in-law.*

✦ *Some fathers-in-law would prefer dental surgery to making small talk. If your father-in-law is the quiet type, don't be disappointed if all you get is a few grunts and nods. When he does speak, keep your ears open; often the best wisdom comes from the men with the fewest words.*

✦ Rent some old Andy Griffith *episodes and watch them together. If that doesn't work, try some Lewis Grizzard books. Works (almost) every time.*

✦ *Goodness gracious, if you can smile through his jokes, you can smile through anything. You know, the one where the string ties a knot around his middle and musses up his ends before walking into a bar, and when the bartender asks him if he's a string, he replies: "No, I'm a frayed knot." Yeah, you have to laugh at that one, too.*

POPPING THE QUESTION

We've all heard that men are afraid of commitment. I don't think that they're afraid of commitment; I think that a commitment to a true Southern lady is what every Southern man wants in his heart. What men are afraid of is committing to a future they can't quite be sure about. Southern men want to settle down with the right woman. They want to be welcomed home at the end of the day with a hug from the woman they love most in the world. They want children that have his eyes and ears, her nose and smile.

If you want to marry, but the man is not ready, there's no good or easy way to convince him. After all, you want a man who genuinely desires to spend his life with you, not someone who feels that he was rushed or forced into something. Step back, relax, and have a good time with your man. If his moments with you are wonderful—and not filled with talk about when he's going to go out and get you that ring—he just may find he can't live without you. If he still doesn't commit, I'm sorry, sugar, but it may be time to move on. It's better to wait for the right man, or have no man at all, than to be tied down to a man who doesn't really want you.

IT'S THE GOSPEL TRUTH

Although movies and television would suggest otherwise, many Southern women still save themselves for marriage. If you feel that saving this gift for your husband is important, let the men you date know up front, in a ladylike way, of course, that a physical relationship is out of the question. If he shares your values, he'll be more than willing to wait.

If he does commit, the true Southern man commits for life. There are plenty of men out there whose hearts and attention stray the minute they kiss the bride, but I don't consider them true GRITS. Marriage is a sacred thing, and true GRITS take their vows seriously. A wife is a companion, a helpmeet, and the mother of his children. If he took his time getting around to asking the question, you can be sure that marriage is something that he takes seriously.

Southern men love romance almost as much as Southern women do. When a Southern man decides to pop the question, he wants it to be special. When he surprises you with dessert after a special meal, you just might find a couple of carats instead of a cherry on top. He'll slip the ring into your champagne—

then watch in horror as you almost drink it. He'll ask the stadium officials to write his proposal in lights during the big game; yes, that's still romantic, it's just *man* romantic.

Or he won't. As much as they love romance, some Southern men don't make romantic gestures. Some don't like to call attention to themselves. Some aren't organized enough to get together a hot dog with a bun, much less make arrangements with a waiter, a florist, and a string quartet. If your Southern gentleman doesn't propose in a grandiose romantic gesture, know that the romance will be in living with a warm, loving, and wonderful man every day for the rest of your life (even if you do have to wash his socks).

ONE CRAZY LOVE STORY

The Courtship

Andy and I had our first date on Friday, October 13th. That date no longer scares me (or maybe it should!). We had a great time. When I arrived back at work, the phone rang; it was Andy calling to see if I made it back okay. Now that's the way to treat a lady! I knew he was right from that moment on. From then on we had to live the long-distance romance until months later we decided we would get married.

Then one day, Andy called me. It was a Wednesday, and he asked if I'd like to get married at 2:00 p.m. on Friday. The judge had an opening and we could tie the knot. Of course I said yes, how romantic . . . the judge had an opening! I told Andy that was perfect; if it was at 2:00, I could get the kids in to the doctor's office to get their records up to date for their new school.

I hung up the phone and realized I had one day to pack my two children and myself to leave for the rest of my life. And I was getting married to boot! The question popped up that the majority of the women in the world would ask. What in the world am I going to wear?

Our wedding was supposed to be a secret so that no one would be offended that we hadn't invited them, but I called my family for help. I have four siblings, and they would relocate a mountain in ten minutes if I needed them to. We picked out my children's appropriate attire and my sister Bobbie made sure I had a suitable dress to get married in. The kids and I headed to Eufaula.

The Wedding Day

I spent the morning of my wedding taking my kids to get vaccinated. After that trauma, we went to meet Andy. When he presented me with two beautiful bouquets of roses, I finally felt that it was a real wedding.

We went to the courthouse and the judge said she just happened to find a Bible and asked was it okay if she used it. Well, yeah! We need all the help we can get! She began the ceremony, and much to our surprise, Andy's son burst into tears. Those tears started a chain reaction among the other kids. When the judge asked us for our rings, we realized that we didn't have any. We motioned for her to continue and finally she got to the good part and Andy kissed the bride.

The Reception

We pulled up to the most obvious place at this point for a reception . . . Pizza Hut. We gave the kids all the quarters they could stuff into the junk machines and everyone was totally happy. We did splurge and got the side salad in addition to a pizza.

The Honeymoon

The rest is history. Although we have never had a real honeymoon, we are living it. My dreams came true; I have found my true love and we laugh every day. We were made for each other in more ways than one. It's hard to believe that it hasn't been quite four years but it feels like we have always been together. I thank God every day for Andy.

—Ann Sparks,
Alabama

HUSBANDRY 101 AND ROMANCE

Any guy can say "I do," but only a few understand the fine art of romance after the vows are stated.

In the first years of our marriage, "romance" means flowers, candy, cards, dinner, and movies out. Sometimes, your man will give you the appropriate to-die-for fabulous gifts of diamonds and rubies, or even the "knock you outta of ya socks" fox jacket.

Then, as the early years of child rearing, career building, and house buying turn into the mid-years, "romance" takes on a whole new definition. "Romance" moves to the next best phase, or the "almost perfect romance." The "almost perfect romance" means never having to gas up your vehicle (much less take it for detailed cleaning), never dropping off your cleaning or picking it up. Forget the grocery store, Mr. "Almost Perfect Romance" handles groceries (buying and unloading and putting them in the proper place in the pantry). When the rain comes fast and hard, or if it is merely a light sprinkling, that sweet man holds your um-

brella from the house to the car, and you never have to touch a door handle again.

Moving from "romance" to the "almost perfect romance" to the "perfected romance" is like waiting for a vintage wine to age. It takes its own time, does so quietly, and most of time without fanfare or flash bulbs, but it is perfected just the same. "Perfected romance" is an art form all its own. Walking through the door in the evening, your drink is made, your bath water started, and you have an hour all to yourself for soaking and unwinding while you sip that drink slowly and breathe deeply. Step out of that tub, wrap up in your favorite jammies, and sit quietly with the man you love over a simple dinner seasoned with much laughter. At the end of the evening, he holds your hands and says, "You're the best friend I have, I would marry you all over again!"

That, my friend, is "perfected romance" truly defined. How do I know? I married him. After all these years, I have "romance," "almost perfect romance," and "perfected romance" day in and day out. His name is Keith Parker and I am not only the happiest, most in-love, and loved woman, but also the most perfectly spoiled woman on earth.

—Paula Parker,
Texas

HOME SWEET HOME

Whether you are tying the knot or just shacking up (though your Southern mother would not approve!), there comes a time when a man and a woman make a home together. Whether he's moving into your home or you're moving into his, there are a few simple ways to make the transition easier.

* *Everyone accumulates mementos, and this is particularly true if your husband has been married before. If he has family photographs, trophies, or homemade gifts from his children, make a space for them on the wall or the shelf. If he's letting his family memories sit in a drawer, surprise him by framing a few. Now, I'm not suggesting that you place photos of his ex-wife on the mantelpiece, honey, but special memories of his children and his family will help to bring a piece of him into your new life together.*

* *If you are moving into your husband's home, respect that he may be a bit uncomfortable at first. Remember, training an older man is as hard as training an older dog, and quick change may make him nervous. While you should be able to bring in your own furniture and mementos, be respectful. Before pulling down the wallpaper or throwing out his baseball cap collection, consult with him, and be sure that you both are happy with the renovations. After all, you may be losing an antique credenza, but you're gaining a wonderful Southern gentleman.*

* *Wedding guests usually want to give gifts, even for a second (or third) marriage. When two people with established lives marry, however, there's no need for yet another blender or toaster . . .*

although any Southern girl worth her pearls could always use another set of china. It is acceptable to say that you would love a gift to your favorite charity, or to say that you'd like nothing more than the wonderful pleasure of their company. As an alternative, collect gifts for a local orphanage or woman's shelter. Ask for toys, clothing, and household goods, then drop the gifts off before your honeymoon. Guests will have the pleasure of shopping for a personal gift, and everyone can feel good knowing that they are helping someone in need. Please don't note these alternative gift preferences on your invitation—that's just tacky—but if your guests ask what you want, don't hesitate to tell them.

✦ Decorating doesn't have a reputation for being particularly manly, so many men would rather spend an afternoon crying over Steel Magnolias than admit they know the difference between chintz and tulle. In spite of what they say, however, most men notice the way their home looks. When you're decorating, ask for your husband's input. If he doesn't want to stare at carpet samples or paint swatches for hours, try to keep his tastes in mind while you do the choosing. Painting the living room pink and reupholstering the sofa in a rosebud pattern may look lovely, but it is hardly masculine. When decorating for two, bring in masculine shapes, such as sturdy furniture and clean lines, and manly colors—neutrals, earth tones, and primary colors. Fluffy pillows and pastels have the place in the home, just not next to the old La-Z-Boy.

✦ We Southerners treasure our own little patch of green, even if it's nothing but a double-wide and a strip of concrete. Mowing the *lawn, cleaning the gutters, painting the trim, and sweeping the steps are not, however, everyone's cup of tea. Remember that there's no rule saying that every family has to own a home and a lawn. There are almost endless options for Southerners today: condos, cluster homes, rental apartments, retirement communities. If you and your husband would rather be working or playing than weeding the garden, explore your other options.*

Whether you're married or not, every woman deserves a honeymoon, but of course it's even more appropriate after a wedding! Many couples feel that they should just skip the trip and make every day a honeymoon together. I say that attitude is about as much fun as scheduling dental surgery for your birthday! It's true that honeymoons can be expensive, but can you think of any better reason for a little splurge? Even if you're on your second marriage, every couple deserves at least one night away from answering machines, dirty dishes, and screaming teenagers. If you feel that a week in Cancún is a bit much for two parents in their fifties, at least reserve a room for an evening at the best hotel in town. When you're back at the house dealing with your everyday domestic emergencies, you'll look back fondly at the night of peace and quiet (or something a bit louder) you spent nestled with your sweetie.

I'M JUST A GIRL
WHO CAN SAY NO

I've had no trouble finding men to marry me. If I have a trouble, it's saying no! If you are a Southern woman, you owe it to yourself and to the man not just to say yes when the time is right, but to say good-bye when the time is wrong. It's hard for Southern ladies to turn someone down, but it's worth it for your—and his—future happiness.

- ✦ If a relationship is not working, it's best to say so politely but firmly. Southerners hate to disappoint, so we hem and haw and try to put things off. Unfortunately, a lot of men are just about as subtle as a big pile of bricks, so it's best to be direct with them. They may be disappointed, but, ultimately, they'll be grateful that you didn't string them along.
- ✦ If a man doesn't take "no" for an answer—and GRITS do like a challenge—speak your mind in no uncertain terms. If he still doesn't take "no" for an answer, tell him that you have a wonderful single friend who'd like to meet him.
- ✦ If all else fails, tell him that you want to get married right away! If a man won't stop pursuing you, pursuing him just might scare him away. If he still won't go away, tell him you're just dying to have lots of children. Men are usually scared of being roped into a quick marriage and family, even if they like a woman. Honey, this works even if you're well past sixty . . . just tell him that you want to adopt.

✦ If he meets your proposal with a "yes," you still have hope. Tell him that you need him to buy a bigger house because your mother and her sisters are moving in.

✦ If he is still interested in you, honey, you might as well say yes. Any man that's persistent enough to build a new house for your Mama is a keeper!

KEEPING THE FIRES BURNING

It takes some work, and sometimes some heartache, but there's nothing more joyful than a marriage that lasts. Goodness knows, I have yet to be in a life-long relationship with a man (except maybe my lawyer!), but I think I've learned enough from my failures to teach others not to make the same mistakes I made. Even with my divorces, I still think that a loving, life-long commitment is worth striving for, and I haven't given up hope.

BEATS ALL I HAVE EVER SEEN!

According to the U.S. government, the South leads the nation in divorce rates. Every state in the South except South Carolina leads the national averages in per capita divorces. The Northeast has the lowest divorce rate in the country.

Many Southern women say that a long-term marriage is about falling in love with your husband again and again (even when he gets on your very last nerve). You loved that competitive, athletic man straight out of school, then you loved the gentle father of your children and devoted family man, you learned to love that handsome retiree who wanted to explore the world, and, finally, you loved that doting grandfather. Marriage is not about passion every day of your life, but it is about finding a devoted companion, and a friend that you can explore and reexplore for the rest of your life. He's not perfect—he is a man, bless his heart—but he's a GRITS worth working for.

DON'T LOSE THAT LOVING FEELING

✦ *Live within your means, and if your husband cannot live within his, make an appointment with a financial planner. Many couples split up over money, and, frankly, it just isn't worth fussing and fighting over.*

✦ *Be positive about your husband. After years together, his little problems may annoy you all out of proportion to their seriousness. When he tracks mud across your floor for the second time in a week and insists on burping "The Star Spangled Banner" after a meal, take a few minutes to think about or write down all the wonderful things about him.*

✦ *"Dahlin'" each other. Even after fifty years of marriage, romance is important. Tell him how wonderful he is every day, and take the time to give him little notes, e-mails, and gifts. Even though you may be surrounded by children or grandkids, try to spend at least one night a week with just the two of you.*

✦ *Always keep it fresh. If you've gone to the beach each of the last twenty summers, suggest the mountains, the big city, or even a foreign country. If you've taken to wearing granny panties, take a chance and visit Victoria's Secret. If you've been taking him for granted, write him a little note telling him how much he means to you. If you're fresh out of ideas, talk to your girlfriends; you'd be surprised by the creative things that Southern women do to keep their men interested.*

✦ *Rely on your friends and family, not just each other. A marriage supported by an entire community, and by God, is always stronger than a marriage that must stand on its own.*

✦ *Face your problems, and don't let them fester. Learn to laugh at the little things and forgive, and learn that there are very few things that aren't little things.*

BEATS ALL I HAVE EVER SEEN!

Some couples believe that marriage is more likely to be successful if they try things out by living together first. Maybe they should think again. Studies have shown that the divorce rate for people who live together before marriage is nearly 50 percent higher than the divorce rate of those who do not. Sounds like couples should listen to their Mamas and not share a home until they share a name!

WHEN A NORTHERN MAN
WINS A SOUTHERN HEART

The best advice I can give ladies out there who either live in the North or married a Yankee is be true to where you are from, never forget your roots, and visit home often. Your girlfriends from back home will be waiting for you with a tall glass of tea or a mint julep on the porch. Don't drive by and miss the opportunity, because time goes too quickly, and once it goes, it never comes again.

I live by my grandma's motto: "Do what you enjoy today because tomorrow things may not be the same." I love North Carolina and my gal pals from back home who truly understand me and what makes me tick because we are made of the same thread. God willing, if it's not high tide in a Nor'easter, I'll go home as often as I can.

—*Stacy Leigh Donohue, Pennsylvania*
(but a North Carolina girl at heart)

Problems will come to every marriage and every life, but GRITS are willing to stick with their women, just as Southern women will stand by their men. Marriage isn't always champagne and roses, but sometimes it is, so remember the good times when the tough ones come. Love your spouse, love yourself, and remember why you fell in love with that dear man. He's a GRITS, and there's nothing finer in this world.

LOVING UNA

One summer in 1996, Leo and Una Watson of Clinton Township, Michigan, were driving through Alabama when they spotted a billboard announcing that they were entering "UNA Country."

"We just had to see this place. It was just too big of a coincidence," said Leo. When they arrived at "UNA Country," they found out that not only did the University of North Alabama share a name with Una Watson, but the campus mascot, a lion, shared a name with Leo.

Leo and Una fell in love with the campus. Although Una was unable to speak because of advanced Alzheimer's disease, she clearly enjoyed herself; Leo had to restrain her from following the students around. He took her everywhere, even in her final stages of this disease—a true love story.

As the years passed, Leo and Una continued to visit the campus, even as her disease steadily worsened. They donated money to help with a new lion habitat and the lion cubs that replaced the original Leo. The cubs were named, of course, Leo and Una.

Leo and Una met at a bowling alley. He asked her out, and, at first, she turned him down. Their friends spent a lot of time together, and, eventually, the two of them grew to be a couple. Leo and Una were married in 1953 after Leo returned from Korea. The Watsons eventually had two sons and four grandchildren.

Una began to show signs of dementia in 1992. Leo took care of her for most of her illness, and the two never stopped traveling and meeting new people. Even though she was ill, Leo still doted on her. She passed away in 2001. He still carries a gallery of photos of her in his wallet, and, if you ask, he'll share his treasure trove of stories about his beloved wife.

Upon Una's death, Leo requested that, in lieu of flowers, friends and family donate money to the new lion habitat at UNA. When he attended the opening ceremony, he was afraid to speak because "I just did not think I could get through it."

The UNA community was glad to see him come back. Says Melissa Green, manager of the university bookstore: "He has worked his way into a lot of hearts around here."

—Elizabeth Stockard,
Alabama

SWEEPING HIM OFF HIS FEET (OR HIS WALKER)

✦ Sometimes the heart is willing, but you're just too darned tired for romance. Increasing regular exercise can awaken you body and soul, and if you do it together, it can bring you closer. Work an evening walk or stroll into your lifestyle, swim laps together at your community pool, or join a coed gym and go together each day.

✦ The most erotic organ in the body is the brain. Exercise it with each other. Read books that you can talk about, go to the theater or a good movie, or visit a museum. And remember, deep conversation is sexy!

✦ In your years together, he's treated you with romance—or at least learned to wipe his whiskers out of the sink—so reverse the roles. Plan a surprise date, and wine him and dine him at the best restaurant in town, or, if he's an old fuddy-duddy about money, do it at home. Buy or make a small present to let him know you care. Light candles, turn the music down, and kindle a flame (or a wildfire!) in your romance.

✦ Staying busy is important, especially after retirement, but don't go overboard. Sometimes, between bridge dates, golf outings, and grandchildren tugging at your hem, you forget to take time for each other. One night a week, pull out the tablecloth and some candles and have a "date" right in your own home, or, if you prefer, schedule something special outside your house together. Woo each other each day of your lives, and you'll find yourself falling in love a little more every day.

CHAPTER 6

THE SOUTHERN BOY AT HOME

"I had rather be on my farm than be emperor of the world."

—GEORGE WASHINGTON, VIRGINIA GRITS

"My second favorite household chore is ironing. My first being hitting my head on the top bunk bed until I faint."

—ERMA BOMBECK

"I don't know a lot, but I suspect a lot of things."

—JUNIOR SAMPLES

Whether it's Sweet Home Alabama or his Old Kentucky Home, for a Southern man, home is where the heart is. The dust on his table might be an inch thick, and the only free surface might be the television set, but he's as comfortable in that ratty old place as a pig in the mud. If they don't care much for cleaning up the insides of their homes, outside, they know each tree and bush, and they lovingly take care of them (or at least pay someone else to do it!).

A Southern man is most relaxed in his own territory. If you need a favor, wait until his feet are up and he's rocking on his own front porch; when all's right with the world, he'll feel more like making things right with you. If you want to convince him of something, he'll be more receptive with his dog at his feet and a cold drink in his hand. If you need to confront him or deliver bad news, do it when he's got his own couch to fall back on. He'll feel more comfortable, and you can hightail it out of there right after.

A SOUTHERN MAN'S CASTLE

A Southern man likes to think that he's king of the castle. He may not spend much time polishing the armor or sweeping out the stables, but it's his own, private little fortress. Sure, the bank may own more of the house than he does, but knowing that a little square of ground is all his own makes him prouder than if he had a grand estate. He may need a bit of reminding that the castle has a queen every once in a while—especially if he wants to plant his garden smack dab in the middle of your front yard—but mostly it's nice to watch him take pride in his little domain.

BEATS ALL I HAVE EVER SEEN!

Almost every Southern man wants to own his little piece of paradise. According to the 2000 census, West Virginia had the highest rate of owner-occupied housing in the United States, with 75.2 percent of the households in the state owning their own homes. In fact, excluding the District of Columbia, all the Southern states topped the national average of 66.2 percent.

IT'S THE GOSPEL TRUTH

His dining room consists of card table held together with duct tape, his living room is a sorry old chair with the springs sticking out, and his idea of home décor is a beer poster. As much as you love him, when you're marrying or moving in with a Southern man, you might wish that each and every thing he owns had a date with the Dumpster. While it's tempting to ask him to throw everything out, remember that one wife's trash is her husband's treasure. When you're pooling your furnishings, be willing to compromise. Allowing him to keep that hideous old chair is a small price to pay to make a home with the man you love. Don't compromise on the beer poster, but don't make him feel that the house is not his home, and let him keep a can or two out of sight in the fridge.

You might want to paint the town red, but, mostly, a Southern man will feel more comfortable at home. Home is where a man is free to smile, to laugh, and to welcome his friends—usually without consulting you first. Home is where a dog waits for his master at the door as if he's the president, a major league MVP, and a Hollywood star rolled into one. Home is where a man can still find hot, fresh food that doesn't come in a paper sack (even if, as a woman, you know full well that he isn't doing the cooking).

BEATS ALL I HAVE EVER SEEN!

If the governor of your state lives in a mobile home, you just might be a redneck. It sounds like a joke, but in August 2000, Arkansas governor Mike Huckabee moved into a manufactured home during repairs to the governor's mansion. The home was no beat-up trailer; the triple-wide manufactured home was over two thousand square feet, and it had all the luxuries of a less mobile house, including Jacuzzi tubs in its two bathrooms. Governor Huckabee showed true GRITS style about his new abode: "Let the people laugh. I think the difference between an Arkansan and some uptight, wound-up Northerner, is that . . . we're laughing with you, because we like the way we live."

For many Southern men, the secret joy of owning a house isn't keeping his money rather than giving it to a landlord, it isn't making a warm, safe home for his children, it isn't keeping up with the Joneses . . . it's power tools. Within weeks of purchasing his first house, a man finds that keeping up a house is actually a whole lot of work, and, if he's a Southern man, chances are he couldn't be happier. Wandering the aisles of the home improvement store, discussing the pros and cons of various drill bits, and exploring the deep, dark mysteries of his water heater will make your average Southern man feel like a kid in a candy store. Even if he doesn't actually ever get around to finishing his home improvement projects, working on them, and, even better, showing them off to the neighborhood men, puts most Southern men into hog heaven.

THE UN-HANDY MAN

Some Southern men have a deep, dark secret: They can't change a light-bulb. What man wants to admit around the barbecue grill that he doesn't know his needle-nose pliers from his torque wrench? If your man is hopeless around the house, but wants to learn, follow these simple tips:

- ✦ Buy a few basic quality tools. I know that big old drill is tempting, but it doesn't do much good if you don't even own a simple screwdriver. Pick up a hammer, a saw, a small set of screwdrivers (Phillips head and flat), a measuring tape, and a level. These simple tools can accomplish many novice tasks, and, if they're well made, he may never need to invest in replacements. When he needs more, he can move on up.

- ✦ If he can stand the ribbing, have him watch a more experienced friend at work. Books can help, but a knowledgeable person can help much more. Besides, who doesn't want to show off their hard-earned knowledge with someone less experienced?

- ✦ Practice. You may end up with shelves that don't quite sit level and doors that never shut all the way, but it's worth the aggravation when you see the look of pride and accomplishment on your husband's face.

- ✦ Encourage his efforts, even if he hasn't gone beyond fixing a running toilet. Ignore the extra paint that he sloshed on your hardwood floor, and focus instead on your beautiful white ceiling.

- ✦ It's never too early to get your man working. Even a toddler likes to help pile leaves and twigs up in the yard, and older boys can help by handing Daddy the right wrench. By the time your boy is ready to move out on his own, he'll be installing a new vanity and rewiring a kitchen at the same time.

✦ Understand that a "three month" project will actually take three years, and learn to live with it.

✦ Just because your husband is helpless around the house doesn't mean that you have to be. Southern girls can handle everything from duct tape to circular saws and still look beautiful. If you know how to maintain and renovate a home, get busy working, and share that knowledge with your girlfriends.

✦ Be sure your insurance is up-to-date. You can never be too careful when you set a man loose with a staple gun.

MUCKING OUT THE MOAT

For the traditional Southern man, working around the house does not mean housework. Cleaning the gutters or edging the lawn are properly manly tasks, but they wouldn't dream of cleaning a sink or frosting a cake. It may be frustrating when you get home late from work only to find that the porkchops are cold in the icebox, your husband is using your bedroom floor as a laundry hamper, and dust bunnies are multiplying on the living room floor faster than real rabbits, but keep in mind that you're fighting years of tradition. Southern men were, by and large, not brought up to use brooms and vacuums, and some may claim not to realize that there is such a device as a toilet brush. Times are changing, however, and many

Southern men have learned that there's nothing unmanly about sweeping a floor, although I've personally never known a man who didn't claim to have "no idea" how to clean a toilet.

BEATS ALL I HAVE EVER SEEN!

Researcher Dr. John Gottman has found that men who share in household tasks are more likely to have active sex lives than men who don't. If that doesn't motivate him, honey, I don't know what will!

IT'S THE GOSPEL TRUTH

If you find yourself working two shifts, punching the clock during the day and then making the house run at night, asking your husband to give you more help may not be enough. The fact is, many men simply don't have a clue about what needs to be done to keep a simple house running. Their eyes seem to have a strange genetic inability to see the dust gathering on the furniture, the leaves on the porch, or the mysterious substances congealing in the sink. Instead of asking him for general help, it is usually better to ask him to help with specific tasks. "Would you vacuum the living room carpet" is always better than "would you help me clean up?" It's easy to get frustrated when it seems that a man may not be pulling his weight, so remember, honey: That poor little dear really is that clueless.

BEATS ALL I HAVE EVER SEEN!

A new trend is catching on in the South: the deep-fried turkey. Although there's some debate about who invented the deep-fried turkey, as with so many delicious (if fattening) Southern specialties, many people believe it was invented in Louisiana. To make a deep-fried turkey, cooks immerse the turkey in a vat of oil. Although many Southern men couldn't find their own kitchens with a compass, the potential danger of thirty gallons of hot oil combined with the need for big, impressive equipment has Southern men lining up to be the Thanksgiving cooks. People up North might laugh at deep-frying a turkey, but the joke's on them; deep-frying seals in the flavor and juices of the turkey. If the man in your life wants to deep-fry this year, just be sure to read the directions on your fryer carefully; no one wants to sit in a hospital waiting room and miss the big Turkey Day games.

If the man in your life is one of those who doesn't know how to turn on an oven, bless his heart, keep trying to help him learn. If he won't learn or won't try, love him for those things that he can and will do. And, sakes alive, whatever you do, teach your Southern boy to do his chores. After all, he'll find himself a good Southern woman someday, and you want him to be trained right.

BEATS ALL I HAVE EVER SEEN!

The average American woman does twenty-seven hours a week of housework, while the average American man does sixteen. Take heart, ladies, it could be worse; the average Japanese man does four hours a week around the house.

SEASONING A SKILLET, BROOKLYN STYLE

When my grandmother, a native of Louisville, Kentucky, passed away, many of her belongings went into storage. My father, a Brooklyn, New York, boy, found Grandmother's skillet, and he discovered that it was coated in rust. He asked my mother what she wanted to do with it, and she said wasn't interested. Not willing to let a fine old pan go to waste, Daddy sanded down the skillet until it was a dull gray.

Daddy called me and asked me if I wanted the old skillet. Being a girl raised in the South, I, of course, replied that I'd be thrilled to have it. I instructed my father on how to season it. I told him that something like bacon grease was preferable to cooking oil. Daddy took my instructions, seasoned the skillet, and sent it to me. He didn't have any bacon grease around, so he just used the next best thing . . . automobile grease!

I'm not sure if there's any hope for Grandmother's poor skillet, but I'm keeping it around. If anyone can help me, I'd sure like some assistance, and, if not, I can always tell a good story about how to season a skillet . . . Brooklyn style.

—Elizabeth Thompson Krieger, Virginia

THE SOUTHERN BOY NEXT DOOR

He's got a big old truck tire in his front yard, but he's painted it nicely and is using it as a planter. He may kick up a fuss and get rowdy with his friends sometimes, but he'll always lend a helping hand with a stalled car. He may have twenty angry hounds yapping out back, but he'll be sweet as a puppy when a child comes around. A Southern boy might sometimes be a frustrating neighbor—not everyone loves the sound of power tools in the morning—but at least you'll always know that he's got a good heart (if not always a good head).

One of the best things about Southern neighbors is that they can get the men in your life out of your hair for a spell. I know you love him, but sometimes you wish he could just disappear for a couple of hours so that you could get on with your business. You'll be trying to cook dinner, do the laundry, and get the children ready for bed—all at the same time, of course—and your husband will be nipping at your heels for attention just like a puppy. Boys will be boys, and so will Southern men, and there's nothing they like better than showing off a brand-new truck or freshly plowed garden. They may say that they need advice or a helping hand, but, really, they just want to play with their toys. When the boy next door comes and asks if he can play, goodness gracious, say yes and earn yourself a bit of peace.

IT'S THE GOSPEL TRUTH

Even the most gifted home handymen can't know everything. A "husband swap"—and, no, sugar, I'm not talking about anything crude or unladylike—can help you and your husband get jobs done around the house. If your husband is an expert plumber, but is hopeless around electricity, he can volunteer at a friend's house, and that friend can work at yours. Pooling the use of tools can save all of you money, since quality tools can cost hundreds of dollars. Poll the men you know, and find their areas of expertise. Once you get a master list of work that needs to be done, and husbands who can do that work, everyone's home repairs will sail along smoothly.

CHAPTER 7

THE SOUTHERN
BOY AT PLAY

"Show class, have pride, and display character. If you do, winning takes care of itself."

—PAUL "BEAR" BRYANT, ALABAMA

"Skiing combines outdoor fun with knocking down trees with your face."

—DAVE BARRY, FLORIDA GRITS

There are some folks in the world who'd suggest that the Southern boy is a bit, well, lazy, but Southern women know that they're wrong. After all, if he comes home that muddy, greasy, and just plain filthy, he must have been working hard at something . . . or at least that's what we tell ourselves.

It isn't so much that they like to sit on their hands and do nothing; it's that GRITS have different priorities than other men. There might be kudzu threatening his very house, his tax forms might be gathering dust on his desk, and he might have taken a few more sick days from work than his health would strictly require, but he's not just sitting around shooting the breeze. He's hunting, fishing, playing, and worshipping. Life isn't just about working at a job; it's about living a rich and full life. And if a rich and full life sometimes requires a rusted-out car in the front yard for a few more days or months, well, so be it.

THE GREAT OUTDOORS

Whether they're bass fishing or chasing gobblers, Southern men who hunt and fish are following in the tradition of their forefathers. While great-granddad may have just been trying to feed his young 'uns, however, most modern hunters and fishers are enjoying the great outdoors and the thrill of the chase. Hunting is not about killing animals; in fact, a lot of hunters photograph their catch rather than killing it, and a lot of fishermen throw back their fish. Some, poor things, couldn't hit the broad side of a barn with a cannon. Hunting isn't always about bagging the prize buck; it's about getting out in nature, about connecting with the land you love, about getting together with your friends and family, and, as any poor Southern wife who's seen the credit card statement after deer season can tell you, about playing with some big, expensive toys.

BEATS ALL I HAVE EVER SEEN!

When Barry Edmonds of Scottsboro, Alabama, bagged an eight-point deer, he was surprised by its huge white nose. Upon closer inspection, he found that the animal had an Old Milwaukee can stuck on its nose. It's possible that the old buck just got a little thirsty, but it's more likely that a man (not a Southern gentlemen) didn't pick up after himself, and this poor animal was stuck (literally!) with his garbage. When well-bred Southern hunters and hikers go out in the woods, they make sure to take out everything they bring in, and, I hope, a fine catch as well!

FISHING FOR A CUP OF COFFEE

We were fishing on the Kentucky side of the Ohio River, and Brent and I were determined to stay up all night with Dad and Leon. It seemed like they always caught the biggest catfish when we were asleep. All night long, they'd sip coffee to stay awake, but without caffeine, we would always fall asleep before the men. That night would be different. We thought.

I don't know what time it happened, but sometime after cooking hot dogs and boloney over our fire, Brent and I both ended up in our sleeping bags. When we woke up, our backs were sore, and the fog was thick. Leon was sprawled out on his lounge chair sleeping under his hat, Dad was sipping coffee in front of his fishing poles, and the fish basket was full. Brent and I sleepily attended to our poles, and Dad filled us in on what he and Leon had caught.

It wasn't long until Leon roused up and started working with one of his rods. After his line was baited and back in the water, Leon eased over to the banged-up metal coffee pot sitting on the makeshift grill made from old pieces of rebar. "Dang! We're out of coffee. Why didn't you leave me some?"

"I thought I'd let you make us a fresh pot when you decided to get up," Dad told him.

"I can't. We're out of water."

"You've got the whole river in front of you. Dip you a little water out and make us some coffee."

Leon looked at Dad in disbelief. "I'm not drinking that nasty river water. I'll just do without."

Without taking his eye off his line Dad simply said, "I don't know

why it'd bother you now, because you've been drinking it all night."
With that said Leon sat down with a disgusted look on his face.

I don't remember exactly how many fish we caught on that trip or
who caught the most, but the one thing I do remember is this: About five
minutes after Dad's revelation, Leon made his way back to the coffee pot,
slowly dipped it into the river, and in no time at all, he and Dad were
drinking fresh coffee.

—Bryan Auxier,
Kentucky GRITS

Getting out in the great outdoors doesn't always mean
hunting and fishing. Plenty of Southern men have never
touched a gun or a fishing line, but all of them love getting out
in the woods or on the water. They love to think of themselves
as mountain men, even if the poor things couldn't orienteer to
the minivan in the mall parking lot. Whether they're kayaking,
camping, or just taking a walk in the woods, Southern men
love to get their hands (and just about every white surface in
your home) covered with Southern dirt. Even if all they succeed in raising is a bumper crop of aphids, the Southern man
will be proud of his little patch of ground.

THE GARDEN

My grandfather, who we called Pappy, spent a lot of time in the garden outside his Montgomery home. He was most content upon his knees working, praying, and, with humility, allowing God to lead him through every storm life would bring. Not long ago, he died in that garden, with his faithful dog, Patches, moaning by his side. It's now my job to pick the weeds, plant new flowers, and grow a fresh crop in my life the way Pappy did in his. My grandfather was the strongest man I have ever known, and that strength flowed out of a compassionate, loving heart. I remember the last words my grandfather gave to me: "Tiger, it's not the mountain that defines the man, it's the valley of pain, sorrow, and the never-ending small struggles that shows forth his true character." Pappy fulfilled his promise as a gentle, God-fearing man, and was finally ushered into that place of true peace. That's the place I will one day teach my children to strive for, the only place Pappy felt safe: the Garden.

—Pedro Latowe, winner of First Annual GRITS Inc.
Writing Competition, Alabama

IT'S THE GOSPEL TRUTH

An avid gardener shared with me a way to overcome our troubles that is far better—and cheaper—than any form of therapy. She told me: "When I work outside of my home, there's nothing like putting my problems in the dirt and burying them."

PLAYING THE FIELD

Even if he's moved past the couch potato stage, and is starting to send roots down into the fabric, a Southern man will love sports. Friday night wouldn't be the same in Southern towns without football; it's been said that it would be like Catholicism without the Pope. Long summer days wouldn't be the same without endless hours of pick-up softball. And, of course, the roar of an engine means one thing to the Southern man: NASCAR. Now, far be it for a Southern gentlemen (or lady) to look down on someone else for his choice of games, but, let's face it, when it's so cold that lakes freeze, any sane person would get themselves inside to a nice, warm fire. They wouldn't strap knives to the bottom of their feet and go slipping and sliding over the ice after something that looks like a chocolate snack cake. I know some Southerners are enjoying hockey now, but . . . well, I still don't think we should take up sports from the Canadians. After all, people who don't eat real bacon can't be trusted to play real sports.

Southern women love sports, too, of course, but we have a bit more perspective. After all, a Southern girl knows that no matter how important the homecoming game is, it's the dress we wear to the dance that really matters. If the men in our lives haven't figured it out yet, well, remember: they're only men. They're just too simple to understand that the debate between silk and satin will always trump the debate over the designated hitter rule.

BEATS ALL I HAVE EVER SEEN!

College football may be a religion in the South, but we're also a magnet for golfers. Robert Jones, Jr., or Bobby Jones to his friends, was a Southern boy from Georgia and one of the most famous players in the game. In 1934, he and fellow golfer Clifford Roberts decided to hold an annual tournament in Augusta, Georgia. Being a modest Southern boy, Bobby Jones objected to calling the tournament "The Masters." Nevertheless, the name stuck. Today, the green jacket is one of the coveted awards in golf.

IT'S THE GOSPEL TRUTH

"Football is a wonderful way to get rid of your aggressions without going to jail for it."

—Heywood Broun, New York

Southern players wouldn't be the same without Southern coaches. They live for the game, and, even though they can cuss a blue streak when they have their minds to it, they love the boys they coach. Whether he's on a team or in an individual sport, every man has had someone in his life who gave him a hand up, an encouraging smile, or, sometimes, a swift kick to the backside to help him along. If the most exercise the man in your life gets is running to the fridge during halftime, he'll still remember the coaches from his youth fondly, even if he sometimes wakes up in the night with nightmares about running wind sprints.

COACH BRYANT

There are not many days that pass that I don't think about Coach Bear Bryant. He was an amazing man who was totally dedicated to the cause of winning football games, and he had the ability to get everyone around him in that same frame of mind. A major part of his teaching was building character and using lessons learned on athletic fields to relate to problems and solutions in living life.

His ability to influence people and get them to do what he wanted them to do was uncanny. That included not only players, but assistant coaches, staff members, faculty, the university president, trustees, the press, and the population of the state of Alabama.

I was one of those people Coach Bryant influenced. I went from a high school that won six games in four years to the University of Alabama, where we went 31-2-2 in my three varsity years. We played in the Bluebonnet, Sugar, and Orange Bowls, and, in 1961, we won the National Championship.

I learned a lot about winning, and about life, from Coach Bryant, and I wouldn't be the man that I am today without him.

—Bill Battle, former Alabama football player and
former football coach, University of Tennessee,
founder and CEO of The Collegiate Licensing Company

SOUTHERN SAGES

"Don't go to the grave with life unused."
　　　　　　　　　—Bobby Bowden, Florida State University

"Girls, get your purses and let's go back out there."
　　　　　　　　　—Bear Bryant, University of Alabama,
　　　　　　　　　　before a 'Bama second-half victory

"Out of limitations come creativity."
　　　　　　　　　—Dean Smith, University of North Carolina

"One day of practice is like one day of clean living. It doesn't do you any good."
　　　　　　　　　—Abe Lemons, Oklahoma City University and
　　　　　　　　　　University of Texas

"There are two kinds of discipline: self-discipline and team discipline. You need both."
　　　　　　　　　—Vince Dooley, University of Georgia

IT'S THE GOSPEL TRUTH

"To Southerners, football is as essential as air conditioning."
　　　　　　　　　—Dan Jenkins, Texas

HAL SELF

In 1969, my father and I were driving home from signing a running back when a newsflash came across the radio: Hal Self had just signed the first African American to a football scholarship in the deep South. At the time, I was impressed that I heard my father's name on the radio, but looking back, I'm more impressed that he had the courage to do what was right.

For thirty-three years, my father never missed a single day of work at the University of North Alabama. Often, he'd stay late into the night watching game films. Over the course of his career, he was offered bigger jobs at bigger universities, and he probably would have made more money and had more prestige, but he always declined, saying that he had "unfinished business" at UNA. Loyalty meant more to my father than the promise of a bigger career.

Not only did he have his priorities in order, but he made sure that those around him did as well. Every single player who was with him for four years earned his college degree, something that's almost unheard of today. He helped to found and lead the Gulf Coast Conference, and several times was chosen as Coach of the Year. He earned the respect of his peers.

Finally, for fifty years, he's never stopped loving our mother, or his kids or grandkids. It's not all the awards and trophies that fill his case but his character and values that make him a good man.

—Gil Self,
Alabama

It seems sometimes that a man would watch the grass grow if it were a competition. You want together time, and he just wants time to watch a bit of baseball, football, or (yawn) golf.

Why, I've seen the poor things watch lumberjacks saw logs with souped-up chainsaws. Look at it this way: It keeps them out of trouble for a couple of hours, it lets them get their aggression out on something other than the neighbors, and it gives the boys something to talk about other than Southern women.

BEATS ALL I HAVE EVER SEEN!

Some people (Yankees, no doubt) think of NASCAR fans as a bunch of beer-swilling, toothless country boys. Well, think again! NASCAR is, in fact, a sport all Southern men love: Sixty percent of fans are men, and the largest group of fans is Southern. Still, 42 percent of NASCAR fans earn over fifty thousand dollars a year.

THE MERRY FOOTBALL WIDOW

+ *Give a man the space and time to watch or play sports. You wouldn't want him to take away your precious time with your hairdresser, so don't take away something he treasures. Besides, it's more time for you to do your nails, read your favorite book, or catch up with friends and family.*

+ *Shopping for men is never easy—socks are boring, cologne is girly, he's got enough golf balls to last until the second coming, and ties, well, there's nothing good to say about giving a tie. While your friends fret about finding the perfect Christmas or birthday gifts for their men, you never have to worry. There's always a spot in a sport fan's heart for one more giant foam rubber hand.*

+ *Unless his house, his son, his car, or all of the above are on fire, don't interrupt a man during the "big game." And, yes, somehow every game is the "big game."*

✤ *You're a Rambling Wreck from Georgia Tech, but your son just got his acceptance letter from the Georgia Bulldogs. You cheer for 'Bama, but your husband is an Auburn engineer. You love those Tarheels, but your father is a true Blue Devil. When your man is on the wrong side of the stadium, take heart. Except for a couple of hours here and there, you can still have true love. Just remember to keep the trash talking on the couch and out of the bed. Cheer as loud as you want during the game, but keep the gloating, or crying, to a minimum after the final buzzer. And if he just can't keep that big old mouth shut when your team loses, remember, it's just because his school has nothing else to brag about.*

✤ *There are some men who will watch anything, from arena football to curling, if sports are vaguely involved. If he's sat on the couch for so long that the cushion is threatening to merge with his backside and he's starting to find televised bowling interesting, it may be time to drag him away. Instead of nagging, attract his interest elsewhere. Buy him a new golf club, invite over the grandkids, or try on your new, and I'm sure, tasteful, purchase from Victoria's Secret. Show him there's more to life than the thrill of a new lure on his favorite bass fishing show.*

✤ *Use his love of sports as an opportunity to build your family. Challenge him to teach the fundamentals to your children—both sons and daughters. Watch the games together, or, better yet, get out in the yard and throw the ball around. Not only will he and the kids get more exercise, but your children will have memories of Daddy that will last a lifetime.*

✤ *If you can't beat him, join him.*

FOOT WASHING AND
SNAKE HANDLING

Anyone who's ever snoozed through a Northern worship service might think it a bit peculiar to refer to religion as "play,"
but to a Southern man, Sunday morning is a foot-stomping,
floor-shaking, praise-be-to-God good time.

When you go to worship, does the same man who can
manage only a grunt when he wants you to pass the ketchup
suddenly jump up and shout "Hallelujah"? Does the same
man who wouldn't even sniffle when his dog died, or, worse,
when his team lost the bowl game, start weeping and moaning
and shouting for Jesus? Does the man whose only words in a
foreign language are "taco" and "spaghetti" start speaking in
tongues? If he does, chances are he's a Southern boy.

DOWN-HOME DICTIONARY

foot-washing ['fŏŏt wôshing] n. (1) *The practice by some*
Southern congregations, particularly in the rural South, of washing
the feet of fellow worshippers. This custom stems from Jesus washing the
feet of his disciples as a mark of humility. Revised Standard Bible,
John 13:4–17. (2) What Jim Bob "Stinky Toes" Johnson in gym
class sure could have done more of.

BEATS ALL I HAVE EVER SEEN!

Living in the South, does it ever feel like there's a church on every corner? Well, maybe there is; according to a research group, over three-quarters of Southerners state that faith is very important in their lives. Southerners are more likely to pray, attend church services, read the Bible, volunteer at church, or attend a Sunday school class than those in any other region of the country.

It might make some Southern women a little puzzled to see their two-hundred-fifty pound linebacker of a husband suddenly weeping and calling for salvation, but most Southern women are happy to see their men feeling the spirit. Southerners worship in many different churches, synagogues, and mosques, and their faiths are as varied as they are. My childhood friends were baptized in the creek outside of a small country church, Reunion Church of Christ. In much of the South, baptism out in nature is still the norm, but today you'll see fancy baptismal pools in many Southern churches. The methods might change, but the feeling is still the same. No matter where or how they worship, what Southerners have in common is that they have faith in something larger than themselves, and they aren't afraid to share that faith with others or to make a little joyful noise doing it.

IT'S THE GOSPEL TRUTH

"Northerners are offended when we ask where they go to church and Southerners are offended when Californians ask what we do for exercise."
—John Shelton Reed, *North Carolina GRITS*

HOLY WATER

When my father, Ed Jr., was growing up in the big city of Juliette, Georgia, one of the big social events of the year was the yearly revival at the Juliette Baptist Church. Revivals were always held in the summer, and it felt like one hundred and ten degrees in that church. Revivals started around seven o'clock and went on for two or three hours, depending on the lung capacity of the preacher. On top of the heat, mosquitoes so big they should have been wearing collars and dog tags attacked the churchgoers throughout the service. Poor Dad had to sweat through the whole thing without making a peep, because there was nothing a boy would be punished for worse than acting up in church.

During one service, the preacher had brought a container of holy water, and he spent a great deal of time, and numerous scriptural references, explaining its significance. In that steaming, hot church, you can bet that more than one churchgoer longed to take a sip of that water, and I don't mean in a spiritual way.

On the pew in front sat Juanita Hardin. Juanita was about fourteen, but she already stood over six feet tall, and she had to weigh at least one hundred seventy-five pounds. She could play baseball better than most of the boys, and could probably beat the tar out of most of them too, and so she had earned their respect.

Juanita was making no bones about the heat. She was whispering about how her dress was sticking to the pew. Up in front, the preacher finally got around to blessing the water. Everyone bowed their heads in prayer. Everyone, that is, except Juanita. While everyone else was looking down, Juanita ran out into the aisle, swung her legs over the rail, grasped the container of holy water, and drained every last drop. She made it back to her seat before the prayer was finished.

When the preacher looked up from his prayer, he saw the empty container of water, his face drained of color. After he was able to speak, that poor preacher went on to say that the empty container was a sign from the Lord. According to Dad, none of the people who had been looking up rather than praying had the heart to tell him differently, and that his "miracle" was none other than Juanita.

Dad walked home with Juanita, and she remarked: "Hey, everyone got what they wanted. The preacher got his miracle and I got some water." When Dad asked her whether she was afraid of getting in trouble, she looked him in the eye and said: "Ed Williams, you're the only one who saw what happened. If I get into trouble, I'm coming to see you." Juanita never did get into trouble, but even to this day, Dad says, "Ole Nita was a good old girl."

—Ed Williams,
Georgia

Even confirmed whiskey-drinking, honkey-tonking, poker-playing bad boys will eventually get into the act if they're Southern. One day he'll be off in Las Vegas, answering the call of the slot machines, and the next day he'll be answering the call of the Lord (if only to pray that his wife doesn't tan his hide). If he's driven the pickup into your rosebushes or let his cheating heart go wandering, you might wish that he'd hear the Lord's calling a bit sooner, but, don't worry, if you stand by him, he'll come around eventually.

GIVE ME AN AMEN!

I was thirteen, and my parents dragged me along to see Uncle Dewey's first time preaching in his own church. Uncle Dewey, a big man, dark from the sun, had been in construction his whole life. During his drinking days, grace came to him during a poker game one night. His call to preach came a week later.

Uncle Dewey was one of the most humble and soft-spoken men I ever knew. Humble and soft-spoken, that is, until he started to preach and the Spirit took hold of him, transforming him into a fiery messenger of God. I didn't have much love for the holy-rolling, heavy-stepping, God-forbid-you-should-wear-a-little-makeup religion of my extended family at the time, but Uncle Dewey was my favorite out of the whole lot of seven uncles and four aunts.

Uncle Dewey's church was a small cinder-block building with stained concrete floors. I made a beeline for the front, where I could be alone, and sat in the second row of seats. They were like folding theater chairs, nailed onto two-by-fours, and bolted to the floor. Uncle Dewey, wearing a black, starched suit in spite of high humidity and temperatures in the nineties, noticed me and leaned over: "Don't you look lovely. I'm so glad you could come." I thanked him, meaning it, and wished him luck.

His smooth transition from welcome to preaching always amazed me. Before you knew it, he had left this world far behind and was deep in the Word. Suddenly, the Spirit would kick in, and everything was changed. Gone was his humble demeanor, replaced with a thundering righteousness.

As they warmed up, the congregation began to respond, hesitantly at first, with just a few quiet amens.

"Can I hear a hallelujah?"

"Hallelujah," a few said.

Continuing to preach, Uncle Dewey stepped, almost like a dance, bouncing and sliding in front of the church, his voice rising, his face reddening. "Can I get an Amen?"

"Amen." It was a small chorus.

My foot found a little space between the front row's two-by-fours and the concrete floor, and I wiggled it around, playing a little. It was a good show, but I'd seen it before. Just then, Uncle Dewey leaped up onto the front row, landing on the chair in front of me. All of his weight, and the weight of the bench, came crashing down on my little foot. "Jesus, God Almighty!" I screamed in pain. Tears steamed down my face as I looked up at Uncle Dewey. I couldn't move. "Oh God," I muttered. The congregation moved in, laying on hands. Uncle Dewey stepped off the chair, and I pulled out my foot, sighing "yes, yes."

The crowed erupted in praise and thanks.

My mother, not a holy roller herself, was thoroughly embarrassed, but everyone had a great day. Everyone congratulated Uncle Dewey on saving a soul on his first day out. It was truly wonderful to see the congregation so moved with love for God, and Uncle Dewey so proud. I shook everyone's hands and received their congratulations, and, even if I knew the true cause, I have to admit, I even cried a little bit myself.

—C. W. Parker,

Georgia

CHAPTER 8

THE SOUTHERN BOY IN THE WORLD

"I am a great believer in luck, and I find that the more I work, the more I have of it."

—THOMAS JEFFERSON, VIRGINIA

"My friend, the artist Tom Lea of El Paso, Texas, captured the way I feel about our great land, a land I love. He . . . said, 'Live on the east side of the mountain. It's the sunrise side, not the sunset side. It is the side to see the day that is coming, not to see the day that has gone.' Americans live on the sunrise side of the mountain, the night is passing, and we're ready for the day to come."

—PRESIDENT GEORGE W. BUSH, TEXAS

You'll find Southern men in pulpits and foxholes, on assembly lines and in boardrooms, in steel mills and (though their Daddies might turn all shades of red thinking about it) florist shops. Dealing with Southern men in just about any situation where you might meet them out in the world is easy; after all, men just aren't that complicated, bless their hearts. There aren't many problems that can't be solved with a big old plate of friend chicken and a good playoff game. Still, it doesn't hurt to know how the GRITS are buttered in various situations.

FORTY-HOUR WEEK
FOR A LIVING

Gone are the days when a Southern man had to have a red neck and calloused hands to be a hard worker. Today, Southern men do everything from changing the oil in your car to changing the baby's messy diapers. They may be Ivy League, or they may be trimming up the ivy. Whether his collar is white, blue, or even pink, a Southern man will do what it takes to get the job done.

Now, I'm not saying that a Southern man is going to work on anyone else's schedule. Anyone who's ever hired a Southern boy to fix their roof or trim their grass knows that the poor dear is going to show up on his own sweet time. He means to get there when he said he would, but when he spots a deer out of his window or NASCAR is on the television, well, what's a good old boy to do? He's not averse to taking a little break here and there during the day, especially if it's football season. He may take a few hours to go fishing or run an errand for his girlfriend, but you can trust that he'll get things done eventually. That slow Southern pace might drive some Northerners to distraction, but somehow we've managed to get things done over the years, and you can depend on your Southern worker doing the same.

DOWN-HOME DICTIONARY

blue collar [blü kä-lə] adj. *A good old boy doing what he does best. Whether our homes have eighteen bedrooms or eighteen wheels, Southerners have a special place in their hearts for the men whose labor makes this country work.*

white collar [hwit kä-lə] adj. *A new-style Southern man: he works in an office, but he still gets a hankering for pig's feet and home-grown tomatoes. No matter how much you bleach that collar, you'll never get all of the red out!*

pink collar [pink kä-lə] adj. *Even though self-respecting Southern men don't prance around wearing pink shirts (he'll swear it's coral 'til his dying day), there are Southern men who work as proofreaders, bank tellers, and day-care workers. He'll hold his head high as he works—even though he'll swear up and down that he's an "executive assistant" rather than a secretary.*

BEATS ALL I HAVE EVER SEEN!

Everyone knows that real fried chicken takes a genuine cast-iron skillet, a loving hand, and time. When time is short, though, even we Southerners sometimes turn to the bucket. Colonel Harland Sanders brought his secret recipe, and a bit of Southern flavor, to the world by using the then new-fangled pressure cooker to make the chicken people remembered from their childhood in only minutes. When the highway bypassed his town of Corbin, Kentucky, he sold off his restaurant, and, at the age of sixty-six, found himself living off a social security check. Not content to give up yet, in 1952 he began traveling the country, franchising his idea. By 1964, there were over six hundred franchises selling his "finger lickin' good" product.

Southern heritage is the farmer, holding the plow behind the mule. He spends his days answering to nobody but himself and the weather, and he doesn't want anyone telling him the best way to run the land that he knows as well as his own hands. Southern men love other folks, but anyone who's ever talked to an ornery old farmer knows that he wants to do what he wants, when he wants, and he doesn't want to listen to some other man's rules.

While plenty of Southern men work for big corporations, it's the dream of many GRITS to run his own company. A Southern man will work hard for someone else, but he'll also daydream sometimes of packing it all up and taking care of his family with nothing but his wits. Some Southern men don't want to depend upon an employer; they want to depend upon their own hands and hearts. A true Southern man is happier making change for boiled peanuts by the side of the road than making million-dollar deals for someone else.

MAKING IT

My father dropped out of high school during his senior year. After he earned his GED, he began working as a furniture warehouse manager, and he kept that job for sixteen years. He worked hard during those years, and he learned to repair and touch up furniture.

After a few years of planning, he opened up Muns Furniture Repair, and he began to do those things that he had learned in the furniture warehouse for himself. He was taking a big risk; he hadn't graduated from high school or college. In spite of this disadvantage, his business did better than anyone could have expected, and even in his first year, he made a profit.

Sixteen years later, my father still has his business. There have been tough times, but he has kept the business going. My father puts his best into every single job. He's overcome a lot in his life to become what he is today, and he has taught me, through example, what it means to be proud of yourself and who you are.

—Stephanie Muns,
Alabama

WORKING NINE-TO-FIVE

✦ *Southern ladies love to take care of other people, but if you want to be an equal in the workplace, try not to dote over the men in your office too much, no matter how sloppy their workspace gets or how much their ties need straightening. I don't have to tell Southern girls that they don't need to act like men—goodness, no Southern lady worth her high heels would even dream of wearing a man's suit or cussing in the office—but they should try to act professionally.*

✦ *Make it easier for men to treat you as an equal by keeping the domestic arts out of the workplace. If you bake, keep the treats that you bring into the office to a minimum. Hand-crafted goods may make your workspace homier, but they also make you seem like Grandma Moses. Bring those wonderful homemade things somewhere else; the loss to your coworkers is the gain of your family, the neighborhood children, and the people at your place of worship.*

✦ *A Southern man is a boss's dream . . . as long as you remember to keep a civil tongue in your head. If you want your Southern employee to stay happy, remember to treat him with respect. Don't talk down to him—that slow drawl doesn't mean that his mind is slow.*

✦ *Honey, have mercy on those poor Southern boys, and don't make them swoon at the office. Keep professional attire professional. Makeup and jewelry should be conservative and tastefully limited. Short skirts and high heels are wonderful in their place, and, goodness gracious, we Southern women love to wear them, but not at the office.*

✦ Office romance is an invitation to disaster. Now, I know it's hard to resist that cute new Southern boy in accounting, the one that fits into his suit like a hand in a glove, drives the bright new pickup, and flashes a smile that could drop a woman at twenty paces, but for every office Romeo, there are two dozen handsome Southern boys who work somewhere else.

✦ Southerners value honesty, so if you make a mistake, be sure that you admit it.

✦ Southern bosses will expect you to work hard, but they want work to be enjoyable; don't be afraid to joke and laugh with your Southern boss. You don't need to flatter your Southern boss, but if you have an honest compliment, he's all ears.

THOMAS SHANNON

Thomas Shannon was born and raised on a farm in Limestone County, Alabama, an area that was impoverished even by Southern standards. The closest town, Ardmore, straddled the Alabama/Tennessee line, and it's best known as an escape route for bootleggers and "private distillers" during Prohibition and after, when alcohol remained illegal on the Alabama side of the line.

Although Thomas had a strong Christian faith, he also wanted to find a better life, and he scandalized his family by working as a waiter at a beer garden on the Tennessee side of the line. To make amends, he took a job selling Bibles door to door in rural Texas. "Sort of like selling freezers to Eskimos," he'd comment.

After college, he was able to settle down to something a little more quiet than selling beer or bibles, and he began a career in education. When he was the principal of an elementary school in Atlanta during the 1950s, he had to assume many other responsibilities at the school. Principals would often be the school's cooks, janitors, and even plumbers. So one day when the water line was clogged, he was out by the schoolyard digging down to the pipes.

The humidity was thick as syrup. Thomas was sweating through his clothes as the children played at recess. When the bell rang, all of the children went inside, except for one. Little Johnny, all of six years old at the time, stood watching Thomas dig. He didn't say a word. Finally, Thomas stood up, wiped off the sweat, and asked if Johnny wanted anything.

"No," he said, and paused. "But you know, Mr. Shannon, if it's not one damn thing, it's another." Then he ran back inside.

You have to remember that in the 1950s, the word "damn" was pretty strong language, especially coming from the mouth of a six-year-old. When Thomas told the story, many people were shocked and asked how he punished the boy.

His response will tell you everything that you need to know about Thomas Shannon. "Punish him?" he asked. "Why would I punish him? Best philosopher I ever heard!"

—Curt Shannon,
Georgia

Jon Rawl, president and publisher of Y'all, the Magazine of Southern People, *wants to bring a distinctly Southern voice to the publishing world. The South's largest circulation magazine,* Southern Living, *is a great publication, according to Jon, but it is about "flowers, gardens, and recipes." Jon wanted a magazine about Southern people. Jon began publishing in November 2003, and he already has a circulation of 100,000.*

PROUD TO BE AN AMERICAN

Only in the South do you see men raising flags that are bigger than their actual houses. They aren't embarrassed to celebrate the Fourth in red-white-and-blue shorts, no matter how funny the poor things look with their pasty white legs look sticking out of them. They celebrate being American with a bang, and, if we have to chase them and their fireworks away before they burn the roof down over our heads, at least we can console ourselves by saying it's for a good cause.

Southerners, men and women, proudly wave the American flag and, when patriotic holidays come around, plaster every available surface with red, white, and blue. If it's a bit much sometimes, and your husband is threatening to paint the garage door in a twenty-foot flag mural, at least you can tell yourself that it's nice to have him taking an interest in home décor. Sometimes GRITS might go a little overboard, buying everything from red-white-and-blue tablecloths, to shower curtains, and (goodness gracious) diapers, but I say going a little bit overboard for America is a good thing!

I might tease our GRITS about a lot of things, but the deep pride I feel for our men in uniform is genuine. Thousands of Southern men and women give to their country by joining the military. Southerners are not afraid to fight in faraway lands, and even give their lives, for their country. Whether their boys are officers educated at the Citadel or VMI—the Virginia Military Institute, sug—or lowly privates scrubbing the decks and peeling the potatoes, Southern families are proud of the service of their children, husbands, and fathers. We all owe a debt of gratitude to our men who fight. These Daddies, business owners, and husbands give up all the comforts of their own lives to make sure that the rest of us can be safe and free.

BEATS ALL I HAVE EVER SEEN!

Major General Joe Wheeler of the Confederate Cavalry had sixteen horses shot out from under him! He stayed in the saddle, so to speak, and commanded a total of one hundred and twenty-seven battles. He was the only Confederate general to later rank as a Major General in the United States Army, appointed by President McKinley during the Spanish-American War.

Growing up, I was taught to admire those who were in the military, and we were always eager to talk about the heroism of our Southern soldiers. I was thrilled to learn that one of my graduate school boyfriends, Trey Obering, has been named the director of the Missile Defense Agency, Office of the Secretary of Defense. I was introduced to him by his parents, who were in my exercise class at the University of Alabama in Birmingham. If there's one way to doom a relationship, it's to have your parents introduce you! Still, although things did not work out between us, I was impressed by his dignity, honor, discipline, respect, and valor. To me, the uniform stands for all those things, and Lieutenant General Obering was a credit to his uniform. I feel a lot safer knowing that he's in charge of our scuds.

THE RUM CAKE

When my brother was fighting in Vietnam, my mother was worried sick about him. She wanted him to have a taste of home, but she knew that just about anything she baked would be rotten and crumbled after its journey overseas. She decided upon a rum cake, which was hard enough to stay in one piece and would taste just as good by the time it reached Asia as it did in her kitchen.

My mother's first problem was getting the alcohol. We lived a short walk from the liquor store, but we argued for hours about who would actually walk through the door and purchase the stuff. Our house was practically in the church parking lot, and no one wanted the neighbors to see us walking down the street with a big bottle of liquor. When no one in the immediate family was willing to go to the store, poor husband-to-be had to go and buy the rum. Finally, Mother had her alcohol, and she soaked that cake in almost an entire bottle of the stuff.

Mother packed the cake off, and it reached Vietnam in one piece. The problem was, so did the smell of the rum. The vapors of all that alcohol that had been gathering as the cake traveled over the weeks were released in one burst when my brother opened the package. According to my brother, the entire platoon gathered around when he opened that cake, hoping to join the party. They thought that he was hiding a big bottle of liquor from them, and they wanted a sip! They were disappointed to see that it was only a cake, but my brother was gracious enough to give a little taste of home to his fellow soldiers.

—Judith Morton,
South Carolina

In many ways, the military tradition in the South is also a family tradition. Daddies all over the South proudly teach their boys to handle their first rifle, and when they grow up, those deer hunters become the backbone of the best military in the world. Mothers worry about their boys, but they couldn't be prouder of their service. Sons, and, these days daughters, proudly follow their fathers into the service.

SECOND GENERATION ARTILLERY

The 36th Infantry Division was a Texas Army National Guard unit activated during World War II. The only non-Texans were those who, like my father, Daniel H. Brown, were draftees sent to replace the dead or wounded. The men of the 36th began to have reunions in the 1950s, and as families started to come quickly after the war, the next generation came to the reunions, too.

Daddy was in B Battery, 133rd Field Artillery Battalion. The ringleader of the artillery bunch was First Sergeant Doyle "Blackie"

Allen. Blackie was a dyed in the wool Texan from the pointed toes of his snakeskin boots to the rim of his Stetson. To say that Blackie embellished the truth a bit was an understatement. He would go from one tall tale to another, and if he would slow down, the men would urge him on by saying, "Blackie, tell about the time we hit Salerno!" or something similar.

My husband, Melvin, couldn't get enough of Blackie's tales. One time, Blackie managed to convince the whole room that Melvin was in their battery. Richard Slack, an oil man and a Texas senator, walked in toward the end of the conversation and said, "You know, Melvin, I don't remember you." My husband, who never lied to anyone, was going to tell the truth when Blackie yelled out: "Why, Slack, don't you remember? He fell in with us around Anzio. We're going to have to check you out, boy, I believe you're getting senile." Slack apologized profoundly, and Melvin laughed so hard his cheeks ached. As the years passed, Blackie told Melvin that he was a member of the group, even though he was "illegal."

The men of the 36th have grown older, and the reunions smaller. The list of the men who have passed has grown longer, and, several years ago, Blackie was added to that list.

A couple of years back, as Melvin and I picked up our registration packet at reunion sign-in, I noticed that my name tag read, "Dianna Brown Murphree, 2nd Generation Artillery." Tears streamed down my face as I thought of how proud I was to be associated with these men. Blackie, I thought, I may be an "illegal," but I know I'm in good company.

—Dianna Brown Murphree,
Alabama

BEATS ALL I HAVE EVER SEEN!

An Alabama family has the distinction of graduating five brothers—the most siblings ever—from the U.S. Naval Academy. "I found the Crommelins to be as gracious in peacetime as these men had been gallant in war. What family has done more for our country and our navy than the Crommelins of Alabama?"

—Rear Admiral (Ret.) and U.S. Senator
Jeremiah A. Denton, Jr., Alabama

KISSING BABIES

There's an old saying in the South that if you shake a politician's hand, you'd better check to be sure you've still got all your fingers when you leave. We've never much liked politicians in the South, even Southern boys. Even so, it seems like politicians sprout up down here like mushrooms after a fall rain. We may not always like or trust our elected officials, but it seems as if Southerners have a talent for pulling up to the public trough.

IT'S THE GOSPEL TRUTH

There's a reason that certain subjects, such as religion and politics, are best not discussed at the dinner table. They're as sure to lead to indigestion as a pot of Aunt Lavinia's "famous" venison chili. If your family does indulge, remind everyone to keep a civil tongue in their heads. After all, you don't want to cause a regime change in your own family.

DOWN-HOME DICTIONARY

scallywag [skăl ə wăg] n. (1) *A white Southerner who supported the Reconstruction government in the South.* (2) *Any scoundrel, regardless of race or region, who betrays his own people. If a Southern man gives up his down-home country girl for a Northern debutante, his field peas for Boston baked beans, and his Braves for the Yankees, he's a dirty, rotten scallywag!*

BEATS ALL I HAVE EVER SEEN!

Based on the 2000 census, Congress is going to see less pork barrel and more biscuits and gravy in politics. Georgia, Florida, and Texas each gained two seats, and North Carolina gained one. States in the Northeast and Midwest had a net loss of Congressional seats.

It seems like we can't get rid of politicians, and maybe that's a good thing. After all, the South's political power has grown tremendously recently. A lot of the South's new power has to do with the region's growing size, but the personalities and hard work of our politicians have a lot to do with it as well. Sure, Southern men wouldn't leave their wallets or their daughters in a room alone with a politician, but they know they can turn to them to bring new roads to their districts or make sure that a veteran gets his pension.

IT'S THE GOSPEL TRUTH

President Bill Clinton, a native of Arkansas, knows why Southern boys are so good at politics: "I grew up in the pre-television age in a family of uneducated but smart, hardworking, caring storytellers. They taught me that everyone has a story. And that made politics intensely personal to me. It was about giving people better stories."

THE PRESIDENTIAL SCORECARD

Lyndon Johnson . . . Southern
Richard Nixon . . . liar
Gerald Ford . . . clumsy
Jimmy Carter . . . Southern
Ronald Reagan . . . Californian, but we forgive him
George H. W. Bush . . . partly Southern
Bill Clinton . . . Southern
George W. Bush . . . Southern

DOWN-HOME DICTIONARY

carpetbagger [kär pĭt băg ər] n. (1) *A Northerner who traveled to the South after the Civil War to profit from Reconstruction. (2) Anyone, particularly a politician, who moves into an area that is not his or her home to gain a personal or political advantage. In the old days, carpetbaggers went South, but we Southerners got our revenge on the North by sending carpetbagger Senator Hillary Clinton, formerly of Arkansas, to take over New York!*

The fact is, as much as we complain about our representatives, we know that our Southern character makes Southern men naturals at politics. Like all Southern men, Southern politicians love gabbin' and grabbin'. It's a small step from shooting the breeze at the local feed and seed to shooting the breeze in the Congressional cloakroom—and both seem to be about avoiding an honest day's work. Southern politicians won't stop until they've kissed every baby in the room (and their Mamas too!). President Bill Clinton was given a homemade pie by a local woman at a rally, and then ate the whole thing in one sitting by himself (without washing his hands, I'm afraid). Now that's dedication!

OLD-TIME SOUTHERN POLITICAL WISDOM

✦ "A stockbroker urged me to buy a stock that would triple its value every three years. I told him, 'At my age, I don't even buy green bananas.'" Senator Claude Pepper, Florida Democrat

✦ "I've seen many politicians paralyzed in the legs as myself, but I've seen more of them who were paralyzed in the head." Governor George Wallace, Alabama Democrat

✦ "If freedom is right and tyranny is wrong, why should those who believe in freedom treat it as if it were a roll of bologna to be bartered one slice at a time?" Senator Jesse Helms, North Carolina Republican

✦ "Gucci-clothed, Jacuzzi-soaking, Mercedes-driving, Perrier-drinking, Grey Poupon Republican." Senator Howard Heflin, Alabama Democrat, speaking of an opponent

✦ *"The poor dirt farmer ain't got but three friends on this earth: God Almighty, Sears Roebuck, and Gene Talmadge." Eugene Talmadge, "The Wild Man from Sugar Creek," four times elected Governor of Georgia.*

✦ *"One of these days the people of Louisiana are going to get good government—and they aren't going to like it." Huey Long, "The Kingfish," governor of and senator from Louisiana*

BEATS ALL I HAVE EVER SEEN!

Everyone knows that voting is a civic duty, but did you know that it can also increase your attraction to the opposite sex? According to a 2004 Gallup poll, 91 percent of those surveyed believed that they were more likely to fall in love with a registered voter than someone who did not register.

SLICK WILLY'S FOREFATHERS

If a man is going to be a Southern politician, he's going to need a good name. Here are a few of the more famous Southern political monikers.

Ellison D. "Cotton Ed" Smith	South Carolina
Benjamin R. "Pitchfork Ben" Tillman	South Carolina
Jeff "Wild Ass of the Ozarks" Davis	Arkansas
James and Miriam "Pa and Ma" Ferguson	Texas
James K. "White Chief" Vardaman	Mississippi
Theodore "The Man" Bilbo	Mississippi
W. Lee "Pass the Biscuits, Pappy" O'Daniel	Texas
Huey "The Kingfish" Long	Louisiana
"Kissin' Jim" Folsom, Sr.	Alabama

SLEEPING WITH THE ENEMY

You want to raise taxes on big corporations, and he thinks that anything but a flat tax is downright un-American. You want to build a strong national defense, and he wants to beat the swords into plowshares. You want local control for schools, and he wants national standards and testing. What do you do when the man in your life is on the other side of the political fence?

✦ *Don't automatically assume that someone you disagree with is foolish, or even that he's wrong (even though he's a man, bless his heart, and bound to be in error). Listen to his opinions. Ask why he believes what he does. Then disagree . . . politely.*

✦ *If he insists on teasing you about your politics, take his ribbing in stride. Men think that if there's anything cuter than a Southern girl, it's a Southern girl who's steaming mad about something.*

✦ *No one—at least no thinking person—agrees wholeheartedly with a single political candidate or political platform. Find something that you agree with, and work together for that cause. The tax-and-spend liberal can walk hand-in-hand with the tight-fisted conservative when they're working together on a common cause, such as improving our schools or our environment. Even if your common issue is as small as improving local trash pick-up, it can be a marriage saver.*

✦ *In the heat of an argument, it is often difficult to make yourself understood, or to clearly make your point. You may be able to list ten good reasons in your head for why you support a platform or candidate, but when you actually start to speak, all you can do is stammer out "Because I said so!" Rather than arguing about your points, sometimes it's better to let others do your talking for you. For something that won't put you to sleep, I suggest Ann Coulter for those on the right and Al Franken for those on the left.*

✦ *Often, the best way to discuss politics is to simply not discuss them at all. You love your man for his sense of humor, his love of children, his fine manners, and his gorgeous smile . . . who really cares about his position on school vouchers?*

MAKING A DIFFERENCE

Though the big cities of Atlanta, Charlotte, and Houston might make you think differently, not all Southern men are out there chasing the almighty dollar. Though Southern men love to make money, and spend it on the Southern girls (I could use a new pair of earrings if you're listening, hon!), they're also giving back to the world they live in every day.

I admit that sometimes lending a helping hand means that he keeps the hunting camp fully stocked with whiskey, but there are plenty of Southern men out there who use their love and their spirits to help others. Now, if we could just get one of these volunteers to pick up after himself at home the way he picks the trash off the side of the highway, we just might have the perfect man!

AN UNSUNG HERO

You don't have to be a famous politician to change the world. It's often the quiet people, those who live decently and morally, that make the greatest difference in the lives of those around them.

A nephew of my friend Pat Speltz died tragically while he was still very young, only twenty-one, but in his short time in this world, he touched many lives. Charles Wilson "Chad" Eatherly never asked for recognition. He was to receive the University of Missouri's Unsung Hero Award, but he died before he could accept the award. Chad made presentations about drinking responsibly to Greek houses and residences as part of his work for the Alcohol and Drug Abuse and Prevention

Team (ADAPT) at his university. He also gave in smaller ways, bringing honesty, joy, and caring to his fraternity, his friends, and, most important, his parents, brother, and sister. The director of University of Missouri's Wellness Resource Center and of ADAPT, Kim Dude, said of Chad in her memorial speech that his gift with people was that he "made them want to be a better man. That was his magic . . . his ability to bring out the best in others."

I wish that Chad had lived longer, and had been able to bring his love out into the world, but the short life Chad lived was a blessing. Chad's high school teacher, Jamie Brother, wrote that some people know how to live in a way that is worthy of God: "Their lives become miracles. Every moment, every day, they live in the presence of the Divine, and with each passing day they become more Divine themselves. And then they're ready; they are ready to be with God." I hope the rest of us learn from this wonderful boy and strive to live our lives as he lived his.

CHAPTER 9

CARE AND FEEDING OF THE SOUTHERN MAN

"Marriage is not just a spiritual communion, it is also remembering to take out the trash."

—DR. JOYCE BROTHERS

"Most women set out to try to change a man, and when they have changed him, they do not like him."

—MARLENE DIETRICH

They're everywhere from the skyscrapers of New York City to the streets of Iraq, and everywhere in between. You can't get away from them, even if you're sorely tempted sometimes. Even if you hide out on a houseboat in Alaska and make your living knitting tea cozies—and you just might be tempted after your GRITS celebrates his sixtieth birthday by buying a motorcycle and getting his ear pierced—chances are, you're still going to have to learn to live with Southern men, since it seems like GRITS are everywhere from Congress to your own front yard. Even if you don't live in the South (you poor thing), chances are you'll have still a GRITS for a boss, a neighbor, or a boyfriend.

LOVING SOUTHERN MEN, OR JUST PUTTING UP WITH THEM

He's a man, bless his heart. As wonderful as a Southern man is, he's going to make a lot of mistakes, poor thing. Your Southern son may invite his entire fraternity over for some home cooking and not understand why you're a bit grumpy. Your

Southern boss may stock the office with cases of MoonPies, even though he knows you're on a diet. Your Southern neighbor may do target practice in the field behind your house until you're running around as skittish as a mouse surrounded by kittens. When it comes to Southern men, their shortcomings are usually foolish, not mean-spirited. Recognizing that, though they might make some mistakes, their hearts are in the right place will help you to learn to love Southern men, or at least put up with their foul-smelling socks.

Living with a Southern spouse means having a gentle, handsome, and honorable partner, but it also means being awakened at 3 a.m. when he goes out to meet his hunting buddies—or being awakened at the same time as he drags himself home from the big poker game. It means having to attend every single game his team is playing, even the preseason exhibition game against the local community college. It means listening to each and every one of his stories twenty times running. He may be distracted; he may "yes" you when he's reading the paper even though he's not listening to a word you're saying, and, honey, sometimes you have to dress in nothing but high heels and plastic wrap just to get his attention.

INVISIBLE

The longer a man is married, the less attention he pays to his wife's appearance. I learned this lesson the hard way when I attended a football banquet with my husband, Dan, the head football coach at a junior high school.

Gaily dressed to match the school colors, I wore a royal blue suit with a yellow scarf around my neck. Feeling chic and slim, I went through the food line in the cafeteria and filled my plate with samples of homemade casseroles, fried chicken, tossed salads, and chocolate meringue pie. Then I sat down at the head table, decorated with potted mums and blue and gold streamers.

After we ate, my husband spoke about the winning season and the sacrifices the football players and their families had made. A cheerleader sitting nearby pointed at me, giggling. Confident she was admiring my outfit, I smiled broadly at her and continued listening to Dan as he introduced the speaker and presented the team awards. After the banquet, several parents and students came to the head table to shake Dan's hand and thank him for his leadership. Strangely, some people had strange grins on their faces when they looked at me, and I couldn't understand why.

The long evening finally ended, and my husband and I arrived home about 10 p.m. As I changed into my pajamas and prepared to clean my face, I looked into the bathroom mirror. On the lower right-hand side of my chin sat an enormous cucumber seed. Evidently, it had stuck to me when I ate my salad.

"Dan," I wailed, "why didn't you tell me about the cucumber seed on my chin?"

"What cucumber seed?" he replied, staring at me. "I thought it was a wart."

—Judy DiGregorio,
Tennessee

GRITS are considerate and would do just about anything for their Southern women, but they'd rather spend a day having a full body wax at a Beverly Hills salon than spend an hour discussing your problems. Your neighbor would rather rake every leaf in your yard than talk about respecting one another; your son would rather enroll in ROTC and burn the midnight oil than discuss his lack of ambition; your husband would rather wine and dine you than talk about the fizzling romance in your life . . . come to think of it, maybe the fact that he doesn't want to talk is a good thing! A Southern man wants you to be happy, and he does respect your feelings, but open and honest discussion give him a bad case of the heebie-jeebies. There are exceptions—after all, Pat Conroy is a Southern boy—but chances are, if he's Southern, he'd just as soon keep mum about your problems.

To get a Southern man to talk, make it as painless for him as possible. Don't expect hours of heart-to-heart talks, complete with tears. Speak directly. Don't accuse, just say how his actions make you feel. "I feel like you are expecting me to pick up after you when you leave your towels on the floor, and it hurts my feelings" is far better than "You treat me like a maid!" Southern men value direct, kind-hearted correction. Either that, or they're just too pig-headed to listen to anything else.

Although you can expect the Southern man in your life to value you, and to want to make you happy, don't expect him to change. Learning to live with your Southern man, warts (I hope not literally!) and all, is part of making a successful marriage. I've learned—through a lot of trial and error, I'm afraid—that we just need to accept a bit of imperfection in one another. Forgive him, learn to say "Bless his heart," and you'll be a lot happier. With him, and with yourself.

THE OTHER WOMAN

If you're going to love a Southern man, you're just going to have to accept the other woman in his life: his Mama. Southern boys are fiercely loyal to their mothers, and even if she thinks that there are aliens living in the attic and the government is spying on her conversations, you'd do well to be loyal to her too. Even if he occasionally makes a little joke about the fact that she wears her curlers until four o'clock, nobody else better utter a peep about that dear lady. Including you. Whatever her faults, a Southern boy believes that his mother is an angel. Like it or not, she's the woman a Southern man will compare every other woman in his life with, including you.

IT'S THE GOSPEL TRUTH

Lewis Grizzard, the beloved Georgia humorist, wrote about his mother's habit of ending conversations with the phrase "be sweet." "My mother's words were so simple. Be sweet. But we aren't sweet. We don't honor sweet. We don't even like sweet. Sweet is weak. Respect me or I'll shoot you. Sweet is weak. No. No. Be sweet. Be kind and gentle. Be tolerant. Be forgiving and slow to anger. Be tender and able to cry. Be kind to old people and dogs. Be loving. Share. Don't pout. Don't be so loud. Hold a puppy. Kiss a hand. Put your arms around a frightened child. Make an outstanding play and don't do the King Tut Butt Strut to point out the inadequacies of the vanquished. Be sweet. The wonders that might do. The wonders that just might do. I can still hear you, Mama." Mr. Grizzard died just months after writing those words. He went to join his mother, and his beloved dog Catfish, but he left behind some words we can live by.

Though a Southern mother is loving and devoted to her children, she's also a force to be reckoned with. Southern parents demand good behavior. A Southern boy knows that he had better wash his hands, say his prayers, and keep his conversation clean. A Southern mother teaches her son to respect others and to always mind his manners. A Southern mother knows that her boy is the finest in the world, and she is only asking that he behave like the treasure that he is.

IT'S THE GOSPEL TRUTH

"A child who is allowed to be disrespectful of his parents will not have respect for anyone."
—*The Rev. Billy Graham, North Carolina GRITS*

If you're the mother of a Southern boy, you're a lucky woman. Sure, he'll put frogs in your bathtub, stash away a jar of lightning bugs under the sink, and use your best perfume for a chemistry experiment, but you'll know that there's at least one boy who will always think that you're the kindest, most generous, and most beautiful woman in the world. Love of mother starts early; my friend Brenda's five-year-old grandson picks flowers for his mother every day. And he'll always remember your birthday, even if that card is a few days (or weeks) late.

IT'S THE GOSPEL TRUTH

Believe it or not, those wonderful, courtly manners we treasure in Southern men are not part of their genes. Unless they're taught to open doors for ladies, never to curse in front of women, and never to address their elders with just a first name, little boys will never grow into Southern gentlemen. When you see a man who behaves like a true Southerner, thank his mother and father. If you have a little Southern boy of your own, insist that he learn to behave like the fine young man he undoubtedly is.

BEATS ALL I HAVE EVER SEEN!

Elvis Aron Presley grew up as a loved and precious child. Throughout his life, Elvis called his mother, Gladys, pet names. When his mother passed away, his words were: "Her death broke my heart, she's all we lived for, she was always my best girl."

Elvis's career took off after his mother passed away, but he never stopped thinking about her. Several years after her death, Elvis said, "There's a lot of things happened since she passed away that I wish she could have been around to see. It would have made her very happy and very proud." Elvis and his mother are buried side by side at Graceland, and the inscription on his mother's grave reads: SHE WAS THE SUNSHINE OF OUR HOME.

THE OTHER MEN

When you take home GRITS, you get several other men in the bargain . . . like it or not. A couple of months into your marriage, you'll stumble down the stairs before you even have your morning coffee, and your father-in-law will be sitting at your kitchen table, calmly gutting fish. You'll find yourself celebrating your anniversary (if not your honeymoon!) with his cousins, brothers, and, of course, good old Gramps. Your boss will get regular visits from everyone from Cousin Randall to Uncle Ephram, and you'd better learn to keep them all straight. You'll peek out of your window on a quiet morning, and your Southern neighbor's extended family will be camped out in an RV in his driveway. If you're going to have a Southern man in your life, you'll just learn to accept the entire package, and learn to love the whole gaggle of them.

Daddy, of course, is the person who taught him to run a trout line, to catch a football, and to tip his hat to the ladies. Every Southern son thinks that Daddy is a hero, and every Southern daddy thinks just the same of his son.

IT'S THE GOSPEL TRUTH

"Daddies make the best friends—why do you think dogs always hang around with them?"
 —*Bill Cosby as Cliff Huxtable on* The Cosby Show

Southern fathers teach their sons a lot of lessons, but they also share with them a lot of stories, and a lot of humor. Southerners know that sitting around and spinning a good yarn isn't wasting time; it is as important a part of our heritage as cornbread and quilts. Sharing a few stories—true or tall tales—is the Southern way of life. It's from fathers that most boys learn the art of the tale, and it's one of the things most boys most look forward to with their own children.

IT'S THE GOSPEL TRUTH

Does your father admire Bear Bryant, Ronald Reagan, Nelson Mandela, or his own daddy? You can tell a lot about a man by who he looks up to. If you want to grow closer to your father—or any man, for that matter—ask him who he admires and why. You might get some surprising answers.

A Southern father had better have a sense of humor. After all, daddies do their jobs without ever expecting thanks. They'll work overtime to make the holidays special, and then their son will thank Santa Claus for his new bike. A Southern father will throw the football to his boy until his arm is sore, and he might even get the wind knocked out of him blocking his boy's practice tackles. He'll spend years giving him pointers after practice and discussing each play with his son while they watch college and professional games together. Daddy will give him pep talks before each game, and let him know that he can play as well as that boy who's twenty pounds heavier. Then, when he finally makes his college debut, the camera will pan to him, and Daddy's heart will swell with pride as he mouths the words "Hey, Mom!"

IT'S THE GOSPEL TRUTH

A Southerner doesn't become a man until his daddy says he's one.

After a while, though, the thanks will come. Southern mothers appreciate all that Southern daddies do. Take a few minutes to thank you own father, if you're lucky enough to still have him around, and to thank the father of your own children. Even if they don't take the time to say so, Southern children are devoted to their fathers. Daddy may have to wait until his children are all grown up to hear that thanks, but someday he will. When a man has a boy of his own, he'll realize the great responsibility, the great joy, and the great pain in the neck, of fatherhood.

IT'S THE GOSPEL TRUTH

"He is the quiet, firm voice in the storm, the man you depend on to change your flat tire, rock your baby to sleep, and grip you tight and close in the rain."

—Faith Hill, country singer and wife of Tim McGraw, Louisiana GRITS, voted America's hottest husband, 2005, by Redbook magazine

MY ANGELS

I no longer think of stars as stars. I lost my only brother, James Marcus White, Jr., at the age of thirty-six in an automobile accident. My father, James Marcus White, Sr., died on February 29, 2004, at the age of seventy-five. When I see the night sky, it isn't stars I see but these angels looking down at me.

I wear an angel around my neck in memory of my father. He was my greatest hero. Zelda Fitzgerald wrote, "Nobody has ever measured, not even the poets, how much the heart can hold." Remembering my father, I know that she was right. He stood by my side, right or wrong, and I could always depend on him. I miss him each and every day.

—Jenny Ming,
Georgia

IT'S THE GOSPEL TRUTH

Southern daddies put their children first, even in front of football. Robert Brazile, Jr., known as Dr. Doom when he played for the Houston Oilers, gave up his career after his wife was killed in a car accident, so that he could spend more time with his son. He traded his position earning more than a million dollars a year as a quarterback for a teaching career in Mobile, Alabama. Said Brazile of his post-football career: "Most athletes invest in a business, but when you teach, you invest in kids. . . . I needed to be a father to my son, and I realized I could be a father to others."

Every Southern father works hard, even if it's just at avoiding changing the diapers! Some Southern daddies rock children to sleep and wipe spit-up, and some limit their fathering to playing. Both kinds of Southern daddies are special. Even if he doesn't wash the soccer uniforms or feed the baby strained peas, Daddy is an important part of each child's life. Daddy passes on his wisdom, his laughter, his good looks, and, of course, his name.

A true Southern daddy will get his reward when the next generation comes. He'll be the hero of every Southern girl and boy: the grandfather. Whether he's Gramps, Pawpaw, or plain old Granddaddy, he's that wonderful man who seems to know everything, and loves you anyway. He might have been a strict disciplinarian with his own children, but when those perfect little grandchildren come around, he's always ready with ice cream and hugs.

IT'S THE GOSPEL TRUTH

"My grandfather taught me to look up to people others look down on, because we're not so different after all."
—*President Bill Clinton, Arkansas GRITS*

My daughter's granddaddy, Frank, was something else! He loved to watch his children and grandchildren play sports, and he attended every game they played, even community games when they were grown-ups in their thirties. My own father died too early to see me play, but Frank came to watch me play volleyball and basketball. I'll never forget Frank yelling at an official who called a foul on me in a basketball game. Most women would have been embarrassed, but I was on cloud nine!

SOUTHERN LIVING

It is a tradition in our family to spend a week in Gulf Shores after school is out. Parents, daughters, sons-in-law, grandchildren, and friends are there for all or part of the week. One year, on our last day there, I awoke early while everyone else was asleep. As I was trying to ease out of the room without disturbing anyone, my twelve-year-old grandson, Kevin, awoke and said, "Hey Poppa, where are you going?" I told him I was sneaking out to the nearby Waffle House, and when he asked if he could go, I of course had to say yes.

As we strolled across the parking lot, we were chit-chatting about what a great week we'd had. The Waffle House was across Highway 182, a busy four-lane road. All of the cars seemed to be hurrying to get somewhere. When a break in traffic finally came, we hurried across the road. I commented on everyone's hurry, and Kevin said: "Most of these people do not know where they are going and when they get there, they will not know where they are." I marveled at such an insight from a twelve-year-old.

As we ate, talk of good times and nice people filled our conversation. Virtually everyone we'd met was from Alabama, Georgia, Louisiana, and Arkansas. Kevin remarked: "You know, Poppa, it is not a sin to live in the South." Truer and wiser words were never spoken.

—Donald Cann, as told to
his daughter, Donna Daniel,
Alabama

THE BOYS

Every Southern man knows a bad boy. He drives a pickup with an ankle-deep layer of cans and burger wrappers on the floorboards. He has a string of exes long enough to fill the phone book of a small town. He would keep a steady job, but he seems to keep getting those tough bosses who want him to stumble in before eleven. And if you know a Southern man long enough, the bad boy will come skulking around, wanting to know if he can come out to play.

You might worry about your husband, friend, or son hanging out with the boys (or, worse, becoming one), but most of the time they're harmless. You'll be worried that they're up to no end of trouble, but, chances are, they're doing nothing more dangerous than watching television and drinking beer. Besides, nothing will make a Southern man want to hang out with someone more than knowing that it's forbidden. Put up with his friends, and, chances are, he'll get up to no trouble at all.

BOYS' NIGHT OUT!

Don't just sit around moping because it's your man's night out with the boys. Make a little fun of your own, and, chances are, you'll soon look forward to getting him out of your hair for awhile.

✦ *It seems that whenever men are around, Southern women end up being maids, cooks, and companions. Take the time you have alone to take care of yourself. Do your nails, give yourself a facial, take a long walk, or deep condition your hair. Better yet, invite over your girlfriends and take care of each other. The next morning, your man will look like something the cat dragged in, and you'll look, and feel, like a beautiful Girl Raised in the South.*

✦ *If you have to stay home watching the kids, make it a break for all of you. Rent a video, order a pizza, and take the night off. Don't be tempted to iron laundry, dust, or organize. Everyone— moms included—needs to take it easy every once in a while.*

✦ *Do something the man in your life hates. Whether it's going to a sappy movie, eating Chinese food, watching gymnastics, or chatting for hours with your best friend, Mabel, take the time to enjoy something that really gets under your man's skin. When else are you going to get the opportunity to do something fun without him moping around and spoiling it for you?*

In taking care of your Southern man, don't forget that sometimes the best care you can give is to step away. Men need friendship outside of the home, and so do you. Friendship between Southern men is a lot different from friendship between Southern women. They can sit together for hours at a time and not say a word, and when they do talk, they may only grunt about the score of the big game or the way the fish are biting. But, strange as it may seem, that time together is as special to them as the hours you spend gossiping with your best girlfriend. It's a guy thing—we wouldn't understand!

SAY WHAT?

Listening to Southern men talk to each other is often like listening to a couple of Scottish sheepherders; it sounds a lot like English, but you aren't really sure what they're saying. Here's a few quick translations so you can understand male "communication."

He says: Whoa, been putting away a few too many MoonPies, old buddy?

He means: I love you enough to be concerned about your health and well-being. I wish that you would watch your fat and cholesterol intake so that I can have you around for many years to come.

He says: Hey, good to see you again; I thought maybe you'd up and moved away. So, the old wife finally let you off for the night?

He means: Although it's important to love and respect your wife, it's also important to maintain your ties with the men in your life. Besides, the rest of us are getting jealous that you have such a fine Southern woman to go home to each night.

He says: Uh, is that shirt pink?

He means: I know there's a problem. But is it a girlfriend problem or a boyfriend problem?

He says: Man, I sure love beer.

He means: Man, I sure love beer.

BASIC CARE AND FEEDING

I remember the days when it was clear what it meant to take care of a man. A man brought home the bacon, and a woman fried it up. A woman set the table, and a man said grace. A woman cooked a man supper, washed and ironed his clothes, kept his house clean, and raised his children. A man ate the food, wore the clothes, dirtied the house . . . and solved every problem that came up. Both loved and honored each other and how they went about doing it was very clear.

These days, you can work an office job, never raise a finger around the house, and still take care of your man. And no matter what his buddies might say, he can be a house-husband and take care of you. What matters is not fulfilling some set role; it's making each other feel good. It's being loyal to one another, giving each other love and support, and treating each other with respect. It's standing by each other in good times and bad.

KEEPING THE ENGINE PURRING: THE OWNER'S MANUAL

Learning to keep your man running smoothly takes years of patience, and, unfortunately, there isn't an owner's manual. While learning the nuts and bolts of your man's heart can take years, these tips can at least get the engine cranking.

✦ *Love and respect him for who he is, and forget trying to change him. He's exactly who his mama wants him to be.*

+ Get to know and love his family. They might think that the highest form of entertainment is a belching contest. Or they might sit around quieter than church mice, watching the clocks tick away the evening. Either way, if they're his, they're yours.

+ Feed him regularly, even if he knows how to cook for himself. If you aren't a cook, focus on one dish that he likes, and perfect it. He may not come home to a hot dinner every night, but the occasional perfect pot roast will show him that you care.

+ Honor his toys. You don't have to understand his need for forty different types of lures any more than he has to understand your need for forty shades of eye shadow.

+ Respect his "playtime," and encourage him to spend time out with the boys. There are just some things that he doesn't want to do with you, and, honey, I don't know about you, but I'm grateful that he doesn't want to spend hours with me drinking Coors and debating baseball statistics.

+ Ask his opinion, even if you already know what you're going to do.

+ Let him be right if he needs to be. Allowing him to believe that he made the decision, or that it was his idea, preserves the peace.

+ Learn to say you're sorry, even when you know darned well you were right.

Southern men need Southern women. Most of them, bless their hearts, just fall apart when their wives are gone for a few days. They eat nothing but microwave popcorn, turn the living room carpet into a biology experiment, and forget to change their socks for days at a time. Southern men just don't care about some things that drive Southern women to distraction. He's perfectly happy with a dirty house and two-day stubble on his chin, and without a woman to tell him that he looks a fright, it just wouldn't occur to him to live any other way.

Some Southern men think that a seven-course meal is a six-pack and a side of ribs. "Sophistication" just isn't a word in the vocabulary of a lot of GRITS, bless their hearts. If your idea of a special evening is dressing him up in a monkey suit to go to a fancy dinner and the theater, keep in mind that you may be pleasing yourself, not your man. If he'd rather be home-style than haute, treat your man to barbecue, catfish, and the latest car-chase movie. It may not be champagne and roses, but, to his heart, it's the sweetest thing you could do.

A WOMAN'S TOUCH

You don't have to be a homemaker, or even take on more than half of the domestic chores, to make yourself needed around the house.

- ✦ Clothes: Check that his socks match. Yes, it's necessary.
- ✦ Food: Men can often feed themselves, but, unfortunately, a lot of them think that a "balanced diet" means that their frozen dinner doesn't slide off the TV tray. Try working at least one brightly colored vegetable (and, no, I don't mean bright orange macaroni and cheese) into each meal.
- ✦ Kitchen counter: Men leave the kitchen counter a mess, even when they're washing the dishes! A quick wipe up after he's "cleaned" may be necessary.

✦ *Bathroom: Men are constitutionally incapable of cleaning a toilet. Somehow, they can't even see the grime.*

✦ *Closet, garage, or mudroom: It never fails that even the most spotless Southern home will have that one dreaded place where junk goes to die. It's the repository for twenty-year-old news magazines, dirty tennis balls, and twenty cases of Aunt Martha's chow-chow. Just make sure that it's all in one place— one small place—and totally out of sight.*

✦ *Bedroom: I hope that this is the one place that he'll know what to do!*

IT'S THE GOSPEL TRUTH

"Who can find a virtuous woman? For her price is far above rubies . . . She looketh well to the ways of her household, and eateth not the bread of idleness. Her children arise up, and call her blessed; and her husband also, he praiseth her."

—Proverbs 31:10–28, *King James Bible*

Taking care of a Southern man does not mean, under any circumstances, nagging him. Southern men don't like to be told what to do, especially in the comfort of their castle. You can set that salad in front of him, but you can't make him eat it. You can give him the health brochure from the church blood-pressure screening. Pestering him to lay off the beer or the snack chips will only drive him to do it more, or, worse, do it behind your back. Ask him gently to comb his hair, take off his hat, or tuck in his shirt. If he forgets, sigh and sigh again. After all, wouldn't you rather have a slightly scruffy Southern man with a smile on his face than a well-scrubbed glamour man who can't wait to get away from his nagging wife?

The one exception: no Southern man should ever be allowed to go out in public with his shirt tucked into his underwear.

MY SOUTHERN-STYLE VEGETARIAN

My husband, Clint, is a man of appetites. Once, when our three children were young, I bought six pork chops for dinner. I intended that the children and I would each have one and my husband would have two, but I made the mistake of letting him do the serving. He gave each child a half pork chop and ate four all by himself!

When our daughters became teenagers, they stopped eating meat. I've never liked meat much myself, so I was happy to make some serious changes to our diets. Meat was banished entirely, and we avoided too much fat, salt, and sugar. Instead of steak, potatoes, and a side salad, we started eating stir-fried vegetables, rice, and beans. Imagine my surprise when Clint didn't even complain. He ate a small serving of dinner and never asked for seconds.

One day, I found out why. My husband was driving the family to church, and my daughters were sitting in the backseat. As usual, Clint was following the car in front too closely, and when it came to a sudden stock, Clint had to slam on the brakes.

A can of soda had rolled into the backseat. My daughter leaned down to pick it up, and when she did, she glanced under the driver's seat. "Oh, Dad!" she wailed. She started picking garbage out . . . more cans of soda, and, worse yet, the tell-tale hamburger wrappers. Clint had been eating so well at dinner because he'd already eaten on the way home from the office, then stashed the evidence under his seat.

Clint grinned sheepishly. "Well, a man can't eat nothing but rabbit food," he said.

I still try to watch Clint's health, but I also make more food he can stomach. We have a few cans of soda and snacks in the house, and he's agreed not to be eating a second supper from the drive-through. Our daughters moved out of the house years ago, so they won't complain about the occasional steak, and, as long as he gets some meat now and then, Clint doesn't complain about the rabbit food.

—Ann Winter,
Kentucky

A GENTLE REMINDER

Ladies, when conflicts arise, and they inevitably will, gently share this list with the men in your life.

- ✦ Believe it or not, there are situations in which faded plaid shirts and Levis are not appropriate attire. Check with your wife, girlfriend, mother, sister, or any woman nearby.
- ✦ Your John Deere cap makes a terrific accent piece to many items of attire, but wearing it to church, any restaurant where the food doesn't come wrapped in paper, or your class reunion will upset your woman.
- ✦ Wear pants that fit you—around the waist, not the hips. Keep your pants pulled up, especially when you've been working on

your knees. There's a reason that it's called plumber's crack—
and it isn't pretty. Forgive the coarse language, honey, but I'd
much rather see the words than the deed.

✦ Buy yourself one good quality suit. If in doubt, wear it. The
women around you will swoon.

✦ I know that you're a handsome thing, but don't check yourself
out in the mirror unless you're in the washroom.

✦ There's nothing sissy about taking care of your face and skin,
and for goodness' sake, keep those fingernails clean and trimmed.
If we buy you moisturizer, use it; women hate alligator skin—
except on fine boots!

✦ Many items of clothing are actually washable. Your bedroom
floor is not a clothes hamper.

✦ The only item of jewelry GRITS should ever wear is a wedding
band (and you better not forget to wear it, honey!).

KEEPING A
SOUTHERN MAN HAPPY

Southern men aren't all that complicated. You don't need a big bank ac-
count and years of therapy to keep them happy. If you want to bring a
smile to his face, just try one of the following:

✦ A cold lemonade on a hot day.

✦ Tall heels and a short skirt.

✦ A fast truck and a dusty road.

✦ A dog, a tennis ball, and a little boy to share them with.

✦ A seat on the fifty-yard line and an old friend by his side.

✦ A homegrown melon and a shaker of salt.

CHAPTER 10

CAN'T LIVE WITH THEM

"I don't think I'll get married again. I'll just find a woman I don't like and give her a house."

—LEWIS GRIZZARD, GEORGIA GRITS

"The male is a domestic animal which, if treated with firmness, can be trained to do most things."

—JILLY COOPER

Sometimes it seems like life would be a lot simpler without men around. We'd never walk in the kitchen to discover our sinks have been used to clean auto parts, and have to spend the next week scraping oil and grime off of the backsplash, tiles, and ceiling. When the ceiling under the upstairs bathroom grew damp, we could just call a plumber, and not have to worry about spending hundreds of additional dollars to fix our husband's "repairs." We could redecorate as often as we wanted, and feel free to use flowers and colors to our heart's content. We could eat chocolate ice cream three meals a day.

Even with all the trouble they cause us, we still seem to like a man rattling around. If they cause no end of trouble, at least they also give us a laugh now and then. A home with a man may be crazier, louder, and a sight messier, but at least it's also more interesting. For all the problems they cause, we love our men, bless our hearts. But sometimes, despite all that, our good old boys go bad.

WHEN THE GOOD OLD BOY GOES BAD

If you see two or more of the following, you'd better be on the lookout for trouble. If you see three or more, make sure your insurance is in order. If you see all of them, tape down your valuables and put the lawyer on speed dial . . . your good old boy has gone bad.

- ✤ *His new friends have more hair on their faces than on their heads.*
- ✤ *There's Hank Jr. on the stereo, beer in the icebox, and boots on his feet.*
- ✤ *He starts looking longingly at anything with two wheels and an engine.*
- ✤ *The same goes for blond hair and a tank top.*
- ✤ *He begins peeping out the window to see if there are government agents in the azaleas. If he begins digging a shelter under the patio, give him triple points.*
- ✤ *He trades in anything—car, stereo, wife—for a younger model.*
- ✤ *He gets his ear (or anything else!) pierced.*

LAYING DOWN THE LAW

Putting your foot down isn't going to do much good with a Southern man. The more you talk at him, the more likely he is to develop a sudden, unexplained hearing loss. He wants to make the women in his life happy, but not at the cost of losing his . . . well, he calls it independence. Remember: he's a man, and his pride is at stake, so if you want to change his ways, you have to be subtle. Fortunately, he's a man, so he's susceptible to some good old-fashioned man-handling and man-ipulation.

CHANGING HIS WICKED WAYS

✦ *Bring him around with kisses, not scolds.*

✦ *If he's staying out too late, make home more inviting with home-cooked meals, his favorite videos, or—better yet—a Southern wife with a smile upon her face and something frilly down beneath.*

✦ *When he does do something good—even a bad boy will slip up and be good now and then—thank him.*

✦ *Don't underestimate the power of other men to change him. If he's spending too much time with his rowdy friends, arrange a night for some friends you do like to play cards, watch football, or grill burgers.*

✦ *If he's ready to change, be ready to forgive him. Nothing will drive a man back to his old ways faster than a woman who won't let him forget them.*

Now, I'm not suggesting that a Southern woman should be a doormat. If a man is mistreating you in any way, you shouldn't sit idly by and put up with it. I am saying that men might be stubborn when you break out the whip, but bring out the carrot, and they'll move in any direction you choose.

If you have a young GRITS to bring up, for goodness' sake, train him early. Unlike adult Southern men, you can use the whip (not literally, I hope!) or the carrot as much as is necessary. A true Southern boy will love his mother more, not less, for instilling discipline. Teach him to treat everyone—men and women—with respect and kindness. You'll be doing yourself—and the rest of us Southern girls—a favor.

IT'S THE GOSPEL TRUTH

I moved from Alabama to the Midwest when my son was fifteen and a half years old. He was amazed that the kids around him in school (in a very upscale community) never said sir or ma'am. His teachers loved that he would open the door for them, remove his hat indoors, and address them as sir or ma'am. One day, one of his schoolmates asked him why he behaved the way he did, and he responded, "That is what you are supposed to do and that is what my mama taught me."

—Cathy Quinn,
Alabama

DISCIPLINE, SOUTHERN STYLE

My grandmother was a generous and loving woman, but my father and his brother knew that if they brought home a report of bad behavior from school, they'd have to face her wrath. My father and my uncle grew up in a time when "switchings" were the norm of Southern parenting. Grandmother would make them cut the greenest switch off the tree, and she'd give them a couple of good, solid whacks with it.

According to my father, it wasn't the pain that made the punishment bad. Truth be told, it didn't even really hurt; what hurt was the fact that Grandmother would shake her head in disappointment. "This hurts me more than it hurts you," she'd say, and the worst part was knowing that she meant it. Those boys would hang their heads in shame and go off vowing never to be bad again, though, somehow, it seemed that temptation was always waiting right around the next corner.

Though the boys were both rambunctious (and, in their sixties, still are), the phrase "I'll tell your mother," brought the fear of God into them. Mention her name, and those two little hooligans would sit still, listen quietly, and keep their hands flat and meek on the desk. They'd put away the marbles, stop sneaking raisins under their desks, and even listen to the teacher's endless sentence diagramming. Though the paddle was used in their school, it was never brought out for either of those boys; seeing Grandmother's sad face was a worse punishment than anything the principal could dish out, so the teachers never had trouble keeping them in line.

By the time I was born, switching had fallen out of favor in the South, and I never felt so much as a tap on my behind, though, goodness knows, I probably deserved it. My parents were strict, but Grandmother mellowed once she wasn't directly responsible for the children. Grandmother laughed at most of our hijinks, and she was always sneaking us little treats when my parents weren't looking. Still, one stern glance from her, or from our own mother, and my siblings and I would quiet right down. Disappointing your mother is the worst punishment a Southern child can endure. Though the methods might have changed, Southern discipline is still the same.

—Lydia Norton,
Florida

FAMILY MATTERS

Sometimes, it isn't Southern men who are the problem: it's the father, mother, cousins, siblings, and uncles who are by his side. His mother-in-law is in the kitchen telling you how to make the spaghetti, his cousin is in the living room watching reruns of Australian-rules football, his brother is in your garden plowing up your rosebushes, and everyone is in your hair.

GETTING COUSIN CLYDE
OFF THE COUCH

It's the Southern way to welcome our relatives for a spell, but if the brief visit is threatening to become permanent, it's time to take action.

- ✦ Start your cleaning as early in the morning as possible. Open the blinds, run the vacuum cleaner, and generally stir up dust (and noise) at the crack of dawn.
- ✦ Develop a sudden fixation on health food. Insist that there be nothing in your kitchen but green vegetables, whole grains, and tofu.
- ✦ Cancel the cable, dismantle the satellite dish, and start playing great books on tape every evening.
- ✦ If he sniffles a lot, adopt a cat, preferably a long-haired breed. Better yet, adopt four or five.
- ✦ Have bridge on Tuesday, prayer group on Wednesday, and book club on Thursday. If the cackling of all those old hens won't get him out of the house, nothing will.
- ✦ Set him up on a blind date. If he can't get enough of his family's Southern women, maybe he just needs one of his own.

IT'S THE GOSPEL TRUTH

When you marry a Southern boy, you get a new family in the bargain. Whether that family tree is a gracious old oak or a scrubby pine, it's yours now. Ask his mother and father to tell you about your husband's childhood, and about their own, and learn what makes his family special. Everyone's favorite subject is themselves, and his parents will love talking with you once they know you're truly interested. The stories will bring you closer together, and they'll help you know more about the man you love.

If you love your man, chances are, you'll also learn to love his family. You may not want to live next door to them—or even in the next county—but you'll learn to see in them the things that you love in your Southern man. If his family is a little ornery or just plain mean, keep trying; sometimes the sweetest heart is under the toughest skin. If you keep trying and they still won't crack a smile, it's better to turn the other cheek than alienate a Southern man. After all, they may be mean as snakes, but they're his snakes, and he loves them, fangs and all.

IT'S THE GOSPEL TRUTH

When it comes to family gatherings, the more the merrier. Many couples tend to celebrate with their families separately, but you don't have to celebrate with just your own family or with his. Go ahead and invite both sets of parents, siblings, children, and even crazy old Cousin Jared. You won't have to disagree about whom to spend the holiday with, and neither of you will feel the odd man (or woman) out.

TAMING MOTHER-IN-LAW TONGUE

Some women become best friends with their mother-in-law, and some are lucky to keep from scratching her eyes out. When your mother-in-law, or the mother of your boyfriend, can't find anything nice to say, being a friend to her is difficult, but if you can tame that tongue, it's well worth it.

✦ *Try to remember that it's not necessarily personal; it may not be you that she dislikes so much as any woman who thinks she's good enough for her son. Any woman who tried to snatch away her baby boy would be subject to suspicion. You can bet that the sainted ex-girlfriend got the same treatment you're getting now.*

✦ *Ask her for advice. Tell her that she knows his tastes in clothes, food, and fun far better than any girlfriend or wife ever would. Even if you ignore her advice about buying the plaid Bermuda shorts, she'll know that you value her opinion and her love for her boy. It's hard to dislike someone who respects you and needs your help.*

- *Keep trying. It's hard to invite someone over who compares your cooking unfavorably to cat food, asks if you've gained a few pounds, and rubs her finger atop the furniture to look for dust, but after a few dozen visits, she may warm up to you.*
- *Don't just turn the other cheek; try to meet every unkind word with a kind one. Southern ladies are not the type who try to get back at others; the best revenge is simply living your life well, and enjoying your man.*
- *Never complain about your boyfriend or husband to his mother. As tempting as it may be to whine about the fact that he always leaves the socks on the floor and doesn't know a broom from a brontosaurus, no mother ever wants to hear about her son's faults. Go ahead and let her say whatever she wants about him, but keep your own complaints between you and your man.*
- *If all else fails, wait for the grandchildren.*

If you have a son, you may someday find that you are the wicked old mother-in-law. That is, you will be if he ever finds himself a wife so that he can get to work making you some grandchildren. Remember how nervous you were when you first met your own mother-in-law, and treat her kindly. Even if she shows up in leather pants and a torn black T-shirt, there's probably a nice woman underneath. Try to find three things that you like about her, and take the time to tell her about them. Your son sees something to love in her, so you can too.

BRINGING UP BABY

Sometimes, it seems like that old baby will never stop whining . . . and I don't mean your Southern husband this time. I'm not suggesting that children are anything but a blessing—ignoring the ages between thirteen and eighteen—but I am saying that bringing up your children together can strain even the hardiest marriages. Southern boys are just big bundles of energy held together with a bit of mud and denim.

When he's young, the best strategy is to wear him out. Let him play sports all afternoon, and, better yet, have your husband join him so that you'll wear out both fussy men in your life! As long as his body is active, his mind won't be running around in circles planning trouble.

He'll keep you awake for hours while he's a baby, and, just when you think you can get a good night's sleep again, he'll hit his teens. You and your husband will be tempted to move and leave no forwarding address, but, take heart, these years will pass, and you'll have your handsome, adoring son back once again—even if he's gained a few pounds and you've gained a few gray hairs in the process.

OH, MOM!!!

Your teenage son will give you circles under your eyes, so the least you can do is give him a good case of the squirming fidgets. Embarrassing a teenage boy is as much fun as you'll have for the next five or six years, so take full advantage while you can. Here's how to get started.

- Keep his baby albums handy for any visits from female friends. Sit alongside her and provide helpful commentary, such as, "My, he sure did have a cute little tushy," and "Lord, that boy loved sucking on his binkie."
- Stay active in his school, and chaperone as many extra-curricular activities as possible. Keep your frilliest dress handy for homecoming and prom.
- Photograph and videotape everything. You'll be able to blackmail him about his hairstyle and dress later.
- Tell him how much you like his music, and turn up the volume and sing along when his friends are in the house.
- When he has his first date, tell everyone from his grandparents to your hairdresser. If you can, take photographic evidence to carry with you at all times.
- Breathe. It doesn't take much effort to make that poor boy blush down to his toes.

THE GOOCH GIRLS

Studying design in college, I read of the city of Pavia, a small city south of Milan in northern Italy. Pavia was known for its beautiful cathedrals, its mystery and intrigue. I decided if I had a daughter I'd name her Pavia.

Many years later, I met an Italian girl, Patti Strollo, born in Lakeland, Florida. I tease Patti that in Florida the further south you go, the further north you get. I'm not sure whether I had a true Southerner or a Northerner for a bride, but I am sure that she became a wonderful wife. Two years into our marriage we were blessed with a daughter, Pavia Marie Gooch. A year later we were blessed with another daughter, Umbria Claire-Louise Gooch, named for a province in central Italy.

To celebrate our fifth wedding anniversary, we had planned a trip to Paris, without kids. The week before leaving, we found a third child was on the way. Traveling around Paris, we found our way into Willie's Wine Bar for lunch. The wonderful "Irish" bartender took one look at us and said, "You're Americans, eh? Try this Madiran. It's a poor man's Bordeaux, and you won't be getting it in America."

To her credit, Patti didn't smoke or drink during her pregnancies, but I did justice to that wine. The first bottle was good, and the second was even better. Patti picked up the bottle and said, "If we have another girl we're going to name her Madiran." Nine months later, Madiran Patrice Gooch came into our world.

Then a fourth daughter blesses our family, Aveyron Therese Gooch. The river Aveyron runs through the south of France from Spain to the Riviera. Our names may not be traditional, but I think that they're truly Southern.

—Doug Gooch,
Alabama

FIT AS A FIDDLE

The problem may not be your Southern man, but your fears that you may not have him around for very long. Southern men are often helpless when it comes to taking care of themselves, poor things, and that includes taking care of their health. As the Southern man grows older, he stops growing vertically and starts growing horizontally. He discovers the joys of two hundred channels of nothing, and his finger is getting more exercise than the rest of his body combined. He may still be an attractive man in your eyes, but let's face it: he's developed the physique of the Michelin tire man.

Here are a few tips for whipping him into shape:

* Admire the physical condition of your friends and neighbors. Even if a Southern girl's admiration doesn't get him moving, at least you get to look at some fine-looking men.
* If his doctor prescribes medication, make sure that he takes it. A man can keep just about one thought in his head at a time, and you can bet that football, Fords, and watching the paint dry takes precedence over his afternoon pills.
* Make exercise as fun as possible. Challenging a friend to a game of tennis or basketball is a lot more fun than a grueling, solitary run. If he uses a gym, try to find one with lots of televisions to pass the time (good-looking female trainers don't hurt either). Yoga may not seem manly, but once he finds out that he can see pretty women in all sorts of positions, he may reconsider.

✦ Don't place temptation in his path. A box of junk food in the cabinet is eventually going to end up in his stomach. If your children complain, remember that what's good for your health is good for their health, too. The healthy habits you give them now will save them a lot of heartache (and heartburn) when they reach middle age.

✦ The occasional treat isn't going to hurt him, and it may help. If he's been eating his veggies and lifting his weights, a fried pie or two every once in a while won't ruin his health. In fact, if it motivates him to stay the course, it may actually help him in the long run.

THE GRITS SLIM-DOWN PLAN

Staying slender doesn't require any special equipment or an expensive gym membership. A Southern man who tries these tricks should have no trouble keeping the pounds off.

✦ *Say the following to your wife or girlfriend: "Honey, you sure are looking good lately. I never did like those thin women, and I'm glad you aren't one anymore." Run until she catches you or you're safely across town.*

✦ *Repeat. Your body burns more calories in the cold than in the hot, so a few winter nights out in the doghouse with Rufus should help you slim down nicely.*

✦ *Come home with flowers and a new piece of jewelry. You can't overeat if you never make it to dinner!*

✦ *Forget going to an expensive spa to sit in a sauna. This is the South—try your backyard in August. The downside is that you can't throw a little more water on the hot rocks, but the positive side is that you're unlikely to run into any overweight, hairy men wearing nothing but a towel.*

✦ *For cross training, buy a dog. Chase him as he runs around the house, bending and stretching as you go to catch the trailing toilet paper. Rest. Chase him as he runs around the house with your new Italian loafers. Rest. Chase him as he runs around the house with the family cat. Rest. Let him outside. Rest. Let him inside to prevent the loss of the remaining paint on your front door. Chase him—and the chipmunk he's brought back in with him—around the house. Rest. Repeat.*

Unfortunately, a lot of Southern men think that taking care of themselves, body and soul, isn't manly. Personally, I can't think of anything more manly than GRITS who keep their bodies healthy; somehow, though, they seem to think that we think spare tires are sexy. Encourage healthy habits—gently, of course—for the men you love. Helping him by example is usually far more effective than helping him with advice. Talking at a Southern man won't help change him much, but showing him what good living can do may. He may stick to ribs and sweet tea, but he just may see how happy your diet and exercise program makes you and join right in.

HEALTH MYTHS OF THE SOUTHERN MALE

- Gravy is a vegetable.
- Jogging between the couch and the refrigerator is cardiovascular exercise.
- As long as the food doesn't get up and crawl away, it's still fresh enough to eat.
- Water's for bathing. Whiskey's for drinking.
- As long as you get a salad (macaroni and potato count) from the buffet, you can go back as many times as you want for extra ham and prime rib.
- Driving around on the golf course all day, and breaking between beers to occasionally hit the ball, is the highest form of exercise.

HYGIENE LESSONS

When I first met my husband, he had long hair, a goatee, and clothes so beat-up they threatened to disintegrate in the slightest breeze. His dorm room was a toxic dumping ground. His waste basket was just about the only space in the room that wasn't filled with refuse. The pills on his sheets were the only thing holding them together.

One day, I'd had enough, and I told him that the least he could do was throw away that old pizza box on the floor.

"I'm saving it for later," he said.

"It's sitting on the floor."

"It's only been there two days."

"You'll end up in the hospital."

"I don't want to waste it."

Needless to say, I marched right out with the pizza box and threw it in the garbage.

In our years of marriage, he's reformed his ways. He may not shave quite as regularly as I'd like, and he still has some clothes that might fly right off him in a stiff breeze, but at least he doesn't eat food off the floor.

—Elizabeth Butler-Witter,
Florida

HOUSE-TRAINING
A SOUTHERN MAN

Given enough time and effort, virtually any Southern man can be reasonably house-trained. The poor thing may not ever understand why you worry about a little scratch on your wedding portrait or a tiny ding in your great-grandmother's favorite vase, but he can learn to leave his shoes by the door and wash up before he sits at the table.

The best way to train a Southern man is with rewards. A kiss for a clean bathroom, a hug when he puts his dirty plate in the dishwasher, and a big smile when his jogging clothes find their way into the hamper (or, praise the Lord, into the washer) will go much farther than a frown or a yell when he acts like a stampeding elephant. Some Southern men are not only house-trained, but are excellent housekeepers; if you find one, you'd better hold on to him. You may not ever be able to train a Southern man to clean the house himself—you can't work miracles, after all—but you can train him to make your work easier.

GRITS-PROOFING YOUR HOME

* White carpet is never a good choice in a house with dogs, children, or Southern men.

* Paper plates may not be environmentally friendly (and would scandalize your grandmother), but a Southern man won't chip them or leave them sitting in the sink all weekend.

* In the best of all possible worlds, you'll have your own bathroom, and let him go to town with his own. If, like most of us, you must share with your spouse, keep all of your personal items in an individual drawer or plastic container to avoid your eyelash curler being used as a back-scratcher or whiskers being scattered in your dusting powder.

* It never fails that the expensive cheese, nuts, or dessert you've bought for a dinner party end up as a midnight snack. Don't rely upon common sense or a good memory; you can't expect either one of those to come between a man and his food. Write what the food is for on a piece of masking tape, and then clearly label it.

* If you don't want your spouse using the expensive guest towels, keep them neatly folded away. If not, prepare for red clay and black motor oil accents on your white lace.

THE ROOT OF ALL EVIL

He stands, clutching a purse in one hand and a baby carrier in the other, staring at the ceiling tiles to avoid the eyes around him. He snoozes in a chair outside the mall food court. Everyone's seen him: the poor Southern man who's been suckered into a shopping trip with his wife.

It takes a lot of shopping to keep a Southern belle beautiful, but don't think that the Southern woman's love of shopping is the root of all money troubles in the Southern family. After all, it would take me several years worth of mall shopping sprees to pay for one fully outfitted fishing boat. Southern men love their toys too, and rifles, wave runners, and fast cars are a sight more expensive than high heels and silk dresses.

BEATS ALL I HAVE EVER SEEN!

Studies have shown that couples tend to fight more about money than about any other subject. Men tend to give a higher estimate of family income and wealth than women, and women tend to give a higher estimate of family debt than men. Researchers did not look into actual family finances to see who was correct. I'm not saying who's right, but if you've ever seen a man overestimate the size of his bass, his prize tomato, or certain other things a lady doesn't discuss in public, you'll probably agree with the women.

When it comes to money, everyone seems to disagree. One wants to invest in a mutual fund, and the other wants to take a second mortgage on the trailer and go to Tahiti. One wants to look into government bonds, and the other thinks that lottery tickets are a perfectly valid retirement plan.

Sit down with your partner (if you can drag him away from the television or his workshop for a few moments) and discuss the family's finances. Be specific about your family's financial goals. Don't say, "I want to save enough for retirement," but instead say, "I think that we need to be saving ten percent of our income for retirement." Then, listen to your man, and try to agree on a common goal. If both of you understand, and agree, about what you want, you'll be less likely to infuriate the other with your spendthrift or tight-fisted natures.

You'll both fail occasionally, so have a bit of flexibility and understanding. A GRITS, bless his heart, can't help himself around a shiny new fishing lure, so try to understand his weakness. It's only money, after all, and, besides, if you're understanding of him, he'll be more understanding of your need to spend a hundred dollars of his hard-earned money getting your hair highlighted.

TIGHTENING THE FAMILY BELT

✦ *Treat savings as a real expense, just like your mortgage or your car payment, and you'll be less likely to miss a "payment"— or to resent that you can't get that new flat-screen television.*

✦ *Life wouldn't be very much fun if you pinched every penny, but you should know where your dollars are going. Set aside one week (hopefully not the week before Christmas) to see how much you actually spend. Write down every expense from the smallest fast food meal to the biggest curl 'n' dye. Once you see how much money is wasted, and not truly enjoyed, everyone in your family might spend more wisely.*

✦ *Take advantage of 401(k) or other savings plans through your employer. When money is withdrawn directly from your paycheck, you never have a chance to waste it. If you never see the money, you'll never miss it.*

✦ *Plan a splurge every once in a while. Whether it's a new television, a trip to Disney World, or a tow truck to get that old Dodge out of your flower bed, looking forward to a big, enjoyable expense tomorrow will help you stick to your budget today.*

BEATS ALL I HAVE EVER SEEN!

If you are a homemaker, your husband may believe that he deserves more control of the family finances; after all, he brings in more of the money, doesn't he? Well, based upon figures from the U.S. Bureau of Labor Statistics, he'd need over $125,000 a year to replace all of the services that you perform, like child care, cleaning, and cooking.

I SCREAM FOR ICE CREAM

My husband never met a penny he didn't pinch. When the children were young, we rarely ate fast food, but, when we did, my husband would insist that we buy the largest drink and split it among us. Naturally, being a man, he'd drink three-quarters of it before anyone else had broken out their straws.

If something was a "good deal," he'd buy it, even if it didn't make a lot of sense. One night after dinner, he went to the grocery store for a quart of milk. When he got back, he'd also bought a tub of fried chicken. The store's deli was closing for the night, and the chicken was marked down. Though he'd already eaten a full meal, he stood at our kitchen counter eating that chicken, talking about how much money he'd saved.

What's now known in family lore as the "ice cream incident" was the last straw. It was a hot day, and we were driving down a country road to a wedding. We were already late when we passed the ice cream stand. At the sight of a sign advertising four cones for the price of one, he slammed on the brakes. I pleaded that we'd be late for the wedding, that he'd ruin his appetite for the reception, that he'd mess up his clothes, but there was no stopping my husband. He ran into the store and came out with four cones.

"Hold these," he said, handing me three cones. He pulled out of the parking lot, eating the fourth while he drove.

Since my husband was so frugal, we hadn't fixed the broken air conditioner in the car, and it was stifling in there. The three cones quickly started to melt, and drops of ice cream began to fall on my best dress. I'd look frightful at the wedding, and I hadn't even eaten the darned things. "I'm throwing these out the window!" I shouted.

"Just a minute, just a minute," he said, licking ice cream off of his chin.

A huge drop fell right on my sash. "No!" I shouted. I don't know what came over me next, but I threw those ice creams over my husband and right out the driver's side window.

The small problem . . . even in all that heat, my husband hadn't rolled down the window. Ice cream dripped all over the glass, the door, and my husband's lap. I must admit: I wasn't thinking that straight at this point. "You're cleaning that up!" I screamed.

We got to the wedding with both of us looking a bit stickier than a formal occasion would require, but at least my husband didn't subject us to anymore "bargains," at least for the rest of the week. And the good news . . . he cleaned it up.

—Emily Conrad,
Arkansas

SHUT UP AND LISTEN

You walk into the room and excitedly tell your husband about your promotion at work, your son's report card, or your best friend's engagement, and a few minutes later he drowsily looks up from his paper or televison and asks, "What was that you said, dear?" At the tiniest rev of a custom chopper five blocks away, he might be out the door, but, somehow, he doesn't seem to hear even your loudest conversation.

GETTING HIM TO HEAR YOU

✦ *Wait until he isn't occupied with something else. Given that your average man has the attention span of a bloodhound at a petting zoo, you won't have to wait long, but you'll have only five seconds to get your point across.*

✦ *Speak simply. Speak clearly. Don't hint. Use short words.*

✦ *Don't be afraid to repeat yourself, or to restate your point in a different way. It takes him time to hear and absorb information, so make things easy for him.*

✦ *Be calm and be kind. In a world of loud voices, it's the gentle voice that stands out.*

✦ *He may hear better with his eyes than his ears (as any woman who's ever worn a miniskirt to get his attention can tell you). Try writing your feelings down on paper if he won't listen. Some men are less threatened by words on paper than a heart-to-heart talk.*

✦ *Be patient. It's not personal, honey.*

You can talk to men. Just understand that they'd rather talk about doing things than about feelings. You may want nothing more than a hand to hold and a shoulder to cry on, but he keeps trying to *solve* your problems, bless his heart. Men like to fix things. Tell him gently that you just want to talk, and if he doesn't understand, just walk away and give yourself some time alone. After all, he's a man, and he's just doing the best he can with what nature gave him.

IS HE A TEAM PLAYER, OR IS HE PLAYING THE FIELD?

I've been divorced four times, and three of those times, there was another woman involved. I've hired detectives, had breast implants and plastic surgery, and gone through enough counseling to make every woman in the South sane. If anything good has come out of it—besides keeping a good portion of Alabama's attorneys in BMWs—it's that I've learned that the best way to take care of myself, my daughters, and the men in my life is to take care of myself first.

IS HE TAKEN?

No Southern lady would ever want to be the "other woman," so before you give your heart to a man, make sure he doesn't have any of the "issues" on this list.

- ❧ *He gives you only his cell number.*
- ❧ *He asks you to call him only at work.*
- ❧ *He takes you out only during the week.*
- ❧ *When you're with him, the phone rings often, but he either does not answer or does not answer after looking at the number.*
- ❧ *He's wearing a wedding band (honey, if I need to tell you this one, being the other woman is the least of your problems).*

DOWN-HOME DICTIONARY

dog [dȯwg] *n.* (1) *An animal of the genus species* Canis familiaris. (2) *A man with roving eyes.*

hound dog [haȯnd dȯwg] *n.* (1) *A dog typically used for hunting, usually with long, drooping ears.* (2) *A man with roving eyes and roving hands.*

low-down-dirty dog [lō daȯn dər-tē dȯwg] *n.* (1) *A dog in need of a flea dip and obedience training.* (2) *A man with roving eyes, roving hands, and the numbers of half the women in your city. A flea dip and obedience training wouldn't hurt, but probably won't help.*

IT'S THE GOSPEL TRUTH

If a woman steals your husband, the best revenge is letting her keep him!
—Deborah Ford's favorite advice

BEATS ALL I HAVE EVER SEEN!

According to an ABC News poll, 21 percent of men admit cheating while in a committed relationship, while only 11 percent of women admit to doing so. Men were more likely to say that they cheated to fulfill a physical desire, while women were more likely to say that they cheated because of an emotional need.

DOES HE HAVE A CHEATING HEART?

If you're in a relationship with a Southern man, there are some red flags that might give you a clue that he's cheating. Keep in mind that these are only red flags, and there may be plenty of good explanations, so don't call that divorce lawyer yet, honey! Before you feel hurt or place blame, find out what's really happening.

- ✦ After a decade of blobbing out, he loses weight.
- ✦ He changes his hairstyle.
- ✦ He begins to work out or increases his workouts.
- ✦ He buys new, more stylish clothes.
- ✦ He begins going to the tanning booth.
- ✦ He listens to different kinds of music.
- ✦ He stops looking you in the eye.
- ✦ You find perfume or lipstick on his clothes.
- ✦ He starts talking about needing a change or that you've grown apart.
- ✦ He begins to find fault with you, and may even suggest that you need counseling.

IT'S THE GOSPEL TRUTH

"When a man trades in one younger woman for another, it usually means he's seeking youth. But not so much hers as his own."
—Burt Reynolds, Florida GRITS

BLESS HIS HEART

Many Southern men and women are in relationships that last a lifetime (or just feel that way!). To those people, I say God bless you, and keep up the good work. Southern women learn to just say "bless his heart" and let the problems pass, and they—and their husbands—are happier for it.

A lot of us, unfortunately, may have one or more relationships that fail for one reason or another. Maybe we break up with our college sweetheart when we move to the big city after graduation. Maybe that whiskey river finally did take his mind. Maybe our husband has hit middle age and developed a taste for fast cars and faster women. Whether they've turned crusty, burned, or just plain gone off, sometimes the GRITS go bad. Honey, just let him go and move on!

BOUNCING BACK

✦ *As tempting as it might be to smash the windshield of his beloved Trans-Am, the satisfaction you feel when that glass shatters won't make up for the night spent in jail. Do you really want to sleep in a place where the toilet is within reach of the place you sleep?*

✦ *Don't have a rebound relationship. Feel free to make an exception if Brad Pitt is available.*

✦ *Telling your story all over town will make you feel good only while you're talking. Southern women don't need or want everyone up in their business, and Southern men—even that no good rat of an ex-husband—deserve better. Keep private matters private, not spray-painted over the interstate.*

✦ *Try to keep contact with him civil, especially if there are children involved. You'll both be happier if you can keep out the anger. Besides, you're going to want to call him to tell him where to mail the alimony checks!*

✦ *Keep loving and hoping. After all, a fine Southern woman like you deserves a true GRITS in her life.*

If you do finally find your GRITS, chances are your relationship will last forever. I tease Southern men, but, truth be told, there's no one in the world I love more. So if you don't succeed, keep trying. He's out there, and, chances are, he's waiting for a Southern girl of his own.

CONCLUSION

Southern man is enough to turn this blonde head frosty gray. He can't concentrate on what a woman's saying for longer than a commercial break (and not even that long if a beer commercial is on). He can't remember to put the milk back in the refrigerator, and you can bet your britches that if he does, he'll never find the carton again. He plows up half the lawn to plant a few tomatoes. Southern men are enough to drive a sane woman clean out of her head.

No matter how crazy they make us, though, isn't it funny that we can't stop thinking about them? At the end of a party, the old hens always seem to gather together in the kitchen, and, when we do, you can bet that men are the subject of conversation. And, yes, we do talk a blue streak on the phone, but it's only because we have those Southern men to talk about. We get tickled talking about our Southern men, but no matter how much we tease them, we know that we can't do without them. Yes, we complain, but you can bet that there's nobody we'd rather go home with at the end of the night. I hope that our dear Southern men take our ribbing in the spirit of fun.

I love the Southern man's honor, his honesty, his strength,

and even his faults. He makes me pull my hair out in frustration sometimes, but he also makes life a whole lot more interesting. He's the son we want to tuck into bed at night and the husband we want to wake up next to in the morning. He's a Southern man, and, goodness, honey, he's a peach.

ABOUT THE AUTHOR

Deborah Ford is the author of the bestselling *GRITS® Guide to Life, Puttin' on the GRITS™,* and *GRITS® Friends are Forevah.* She founded Grits, Inc., less than ten years ago and has quickly grown the merchandising company into a multimillion-dollar business. She lives in Birmingham, Alabama.